FORECASTING YO

A unique, simple and easy-to-follow
personal forecasting by non-technical astrological means.

By the same author
SUCCESSFUL CAREER PLANNING WITH ASTROLOGY

FORECASTING YOUR FUTURE
How to Prepare Your Own Astrological Time-Scan

Rupert J. Sewell

THE AQUARIAN PRESS
Wellingborough, Northamptonshire

First published in 1983 as
FORECASTING YOUR LIFE TRENDS
This edition first published 1987

© RUPERT J. SEWELL 1987

All rights reserved. No part of this book may be reproduced or utilized in any form or by any means, electronic or mechanical, including photocopying, recording or by any information storage and retrieval system, without permission in writing from the Publisher.

British Library Cataloguing in Publication Data

Sewell, Rupert J.
Forecasting your future [2nd ed.]
1. Astrology
I. Title   II. Sewell, Rupert J. Forecasting
your life trends
133.5   BF1708.1

ISBN 0-85030-572-1

*The Aquarian Press is part of the
Thorsons Publishing Group*

Printed and bound in Great Britain

CONTENTS

	Page
Introduction	7
Chapter	
1. What Is Time?	11
2. Do We Have Free-will?	27
3. The Horoscope and Space-Time	37
4. Forecasting in Astrology	47
5. The Integrated Life Cycle	56
6. The Life Phases	65
Using the Birth Date Table	72
Life Phases	74
Word Code Reference List	88
Bibliography	93
Index	95

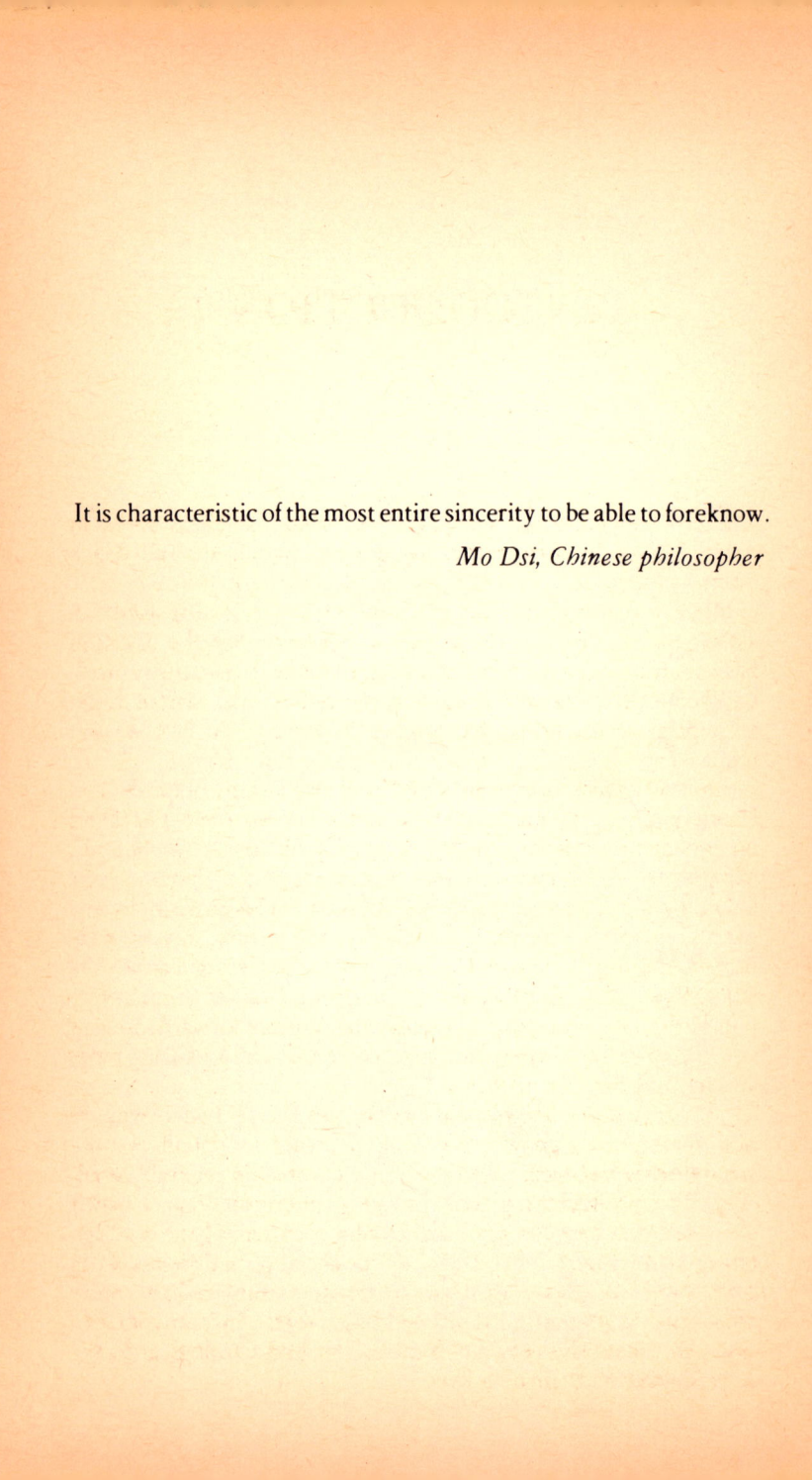

It is characteristic of the most entire sincerity to be able to foreknow.

Mo Dsi, Chinese philosopher

INTRODUCTION

The greater part of an astrologer's professional life is spent in gazing between past and future, along what might be thought of as a cosmic time path.

Inevitably, it is always the precognitive or forecasting aspect of astrology that captures the attention. Students skip the essential basic material because they want to learn 'how to read the future', and some professionals, caught in the public eye, cannot resist attempting predictions that, not surprisingly, do not always materialize!

Some forty years ago — although it seems like only yesterday! — I came across J. W. Dunne's *An Experiment With Time*. His views on precognition were initially prompted by the very common experience people have, in which something that is dreamt about later appears to manifest in reality. When I read that we all have a natural ability to seemingly peer into the future, my interest became thoroughly aroused, and the subject has intrigued me ever since. Eventually, this interest in Time found expression in astrological disciplines, though obviously the mode of forward viewing in astrology is based upon demonstrable factors for measuring time, and not upon intuition only.

For my previous book, *Stress and the Sun Signs*, I had to evolve a new method of sign interpretation in order to obtain a more accurate psychological picture of Sun types than is generally available. When I had completed the list of interpretations, I had it checked by an eminent psychiatrist who eventually gave it a high rating for accuracy. This, and the wide acclaim that the book has since received, encouraged me to try something a little more ambitious; to present a list of Life Phases with which anyone can assess for themselves certain of the established astrological trends or tendencies in their own lives.

However, it is one thing to compile a list of easily recognizable personality traits from birth dates, but quite another if one intends to give a working illustration of the time factor in astrological terms. When one considers the daunting complexity involved in any philosophical or scientific conception of Time, it is hardly surprising that I embarked upon the writing of this present work with some trepidation. Nevertheless, the astrological path is itself well trodden and the theme so fascinating, that who could refuse the challenge!

Then again, it is quite possible simply to consider the last part of this book as being something that offers you an opportunity to conduct a little experiment for yourself. Indeed, if Dunne had not already used the title, I think *An Experiment With Time* would have fitted here very well; although the experiment he suggested to his readers was the rather tedious one of having to record their dreams in minute detail, over a lengthy period. Here, all that is required of you is to read and reflect, and maybe just to make a note in your diary to remind yourself about a coming phase, as outlined in the last section.

One thing that cannot be over-emphasized is that although the list of phase interpretations offers a very simple and easy means of 'forecasting' for oneself, it should be remembered that we are dealing with probabilities or tendencies only, and that these must be viewed within the broad experience of your personal life-style and conditions. Clearly, any attempt to extract meaningful indices from little more than the sun's yearly cycle through the Zodiac, must have its limitations.

Whenever the subject of fortune-telling or 'reading the future' is debated, the question of fate invariably arises. Some while ago, on television, I listened to a discussion on clairvoyance and astrology by a group of well-known personalities and a professor of sociology. For the most part they had no real difficulty in accepting that a precognitive faculty existed, and indeed were prepared to accept it as a natural phenomenon. The professor, however, could accept none of it, and appeared to be excessively disturbed by the loss of freedom of choice which, he contested, such a belief implied. His remarks on astrological research, although indicating a brief study of some current papers, revealed that he had no real knowledge of the subject at all, and I suspect he had only been included in the programme to increase the entertainment value. Even so, his apparent agitation over the moral or ethical issues involved did serve as a reminder, and therefore I have included a chapter on this question.

INTRODUCTION

We live in an age of highly efficient mass communication, yet despite this, astrology continues to struggle beneath a blanket of misunderstanding, ignorance and prejudice. It is not as if there was a shortage of written material on the subject. One reason why a lack of understanding persists, I believe, is to be found in the attitude of astrologers themselves. They tend to write for other astrologers or students, rather than for the general public. Obviously, the main reason for this is because it is such a complex subject, technically, and so full of archaic language that it is extremely difficult to present it in words that make any real sense to the average, interested reader.

And at the popular level, it is the journalist with some superficial knowledge of this ancient science who caters for the mass market, usually in a form of astro-waffle that is difficult to extract any real sense from — even by experienced practitioners!

When I sat down to write *Stress and the Sun Signs* I resolved to keep to a clear and straightforward style, as far as possible, so that the average, interested reader might glean something of value, or at least glimpse something of the eternal truths that lie directly behind the conscious symbolism of all our unconscious motivations. Kind letters from many parts of the world have more than confirmed the achievement of this resolve, and it is my sincere hope that this present work, too, will hold something of interest and meaning for you.

Referring To The Life Phases

You will find a full explanation of how these were developed, and how to use them, in Chapter 5. The fact that they were derived from what was primarily a list of personality and behavioural tendencies is hardly surprising. Our awareness of the passage of time is, after all, an entirely individual experience. Our culture, conditioning and hereditary factors all modify the individual experience of reality. When you come to think about it, even our age effects the impression we may have of time passing. As children, time appears to drag its heels, but as adults we find it slips by at an ever increasing rate!

Procedure For Assessing Your Future Trends

This is quite simple. Ideally, read through the book first so that you may gain an understanding of the general principles involved. Briefly, however, in using the self-forecasting section, the first step is to look for your date of birth in the list provided. Against this you will find a Life Phase number, and how many years the phase applies for in the earliest period of your life. You then move on to the next phase in the list, and so on, as appropriate, up to the current phase and beyond!

Each phase contains key-words, enabling you to refer to the particular section in the Word Code Reference List. This has been specially evolved in order to augment and impart a greater depth of meaning to each of the Life Phases.

1. WHAT IS TIME?

From Aristotle to Einstein theories have been formulated and hypotheses postulated about the nature of time. Bertrand Russell was attracted to the view of absolute time, while Rousseau could not abide the idea of time at all, and derived much satisfaction from throwing away all his clocks and watches!

As soon as one begins to enquire into the mysteries of prophecy and prognostication it quickly becomes evident that what we are really considering is mankind's enduring preoccupation with the concept of time. And time, we soon discover, is a subject that has captured the interest of innumerable minds, both philosophic and scientific, throughout the ages. But so tenuous a subject is it, that agreement as to its nature appears to be the exception rather than the rule. Isaac Newton's view was that the universe possessed some sort of clock; Leibniz thought of the universe *as* a clock.

Of course, differences of opinion can vary considerably, though, for the most part, it is possible to discern two broad groups. There are those who believe that everything must have a beginning, continue for a period, and then cease. This, obviously, relates to duration in time, there being a past, present, and future, more or less clearly defined. Such a belief is founded upon the law of casuality and is readily acceptable to those of a scientific persuasion, as well as to those who derive a feeling of security from the thought of there being some sort of order in the midst of turbulent nature.

The second group consists of those who do not visualize time as though it were a straight line, but rather as if it was an all-embracing 'now'. Here we are at once faced with the complex ramifications of mankind's thoughts and philosophies, but there is no need to make our exploration into the labyrinth of time too complicated, and you will find that the path we shall take is quite well defined.

Sign-posts to the direction of our thinking may be readily

perceived through the medium of popular literature; in particular, science-fiction, which allows plenty of scope for the author's imagination and vision to travel through history, and time. Most of us today are familiar with the imagery employed, because many of the classics in this field have been adapted for the cinema and television.

The writers of these yarns take us into the past, usually through the magic of a time-machine, or through the eyes of intrepid explorers who stumble upon lost cities, either under the sea, in jungles, or beneath the earth. When the writer wishes to take us forward into the future the images conjured up are most often those of space-ships, planets, and super-intelligent beings. Alternatively, the writer may choose to stage the action in the present, and have 'the thing' from the past escape from its time encapsulated, subterranean lair, or have the 'thing from outer-space' visit earth.

What is of particular interest to us it not so much that dimensions of time, even if only as products of the imagination, can be swung from either the past or future into the viable present of the reader's awareness, but the images themselves. These are the things to look at because they tell us vividly and graphically about the direction of the underlying currents of consciousness. Stories alluding to the past teem with images of rocky terrain, caverns, steamy jungles, primitives, monsters of the deep, and so on. Tales alluding to the future abound with high-technology, and the 'stuff' of space. There is a reaching out towards the stars.

Just as the historical progress of religious knowledge has proceeded from eastern society to the west, following the course of the Sun, so does the mystical and spiritual aspirations of mankind struggle from its origins below, in the 'primeval soup', to reach ever persistently upward, into the firmament of the future. Thus, the movement from past to future is paralleled in man's instinctive urge to move from darkness into light, from earth to heaven, or, if we state this in psychological terms, from the collective unconscious to conscious realization of Self, by which I mean the universal sense of Godhead, in whatever way this may be seen.

The astrologer, perhaps more than most, is acutely aware of this cosmic interplay, for the science of astrology is a matrix in which the underlying responses of humanity become crystallized and given meaning. The fact that this meaning is derived from above — i.e. the planetary patterns — should give us pause for reflection, because, as we have seen, above can be synonymous with future. Hence, if past gives reason to the present, then future provides the actualization. In practical terms, this simply means that when the astrologer has analyzed the forward projection of a birth-chart (horoscope), and then puts into words that which is initially seen only as the symbolism of planetary cycles, it is as though facets of the future are enabled to reflect a little of their light upon the present awareness of the listener.

However, before we become too involved with the astrological approach to time, let us take a brief look at the subject in general. Because it is so vast it seemed to me reasonable if it were divided into sections, and the obvious choice of headings for each section is — as you may have guessed! — past, present, and future.

Past

Some while ago I watched a documentary film on television. An archaeologist was talking about a tusk — if my memory serves me aright — dated about 10,000 years. On this was a spiral pattern of dots. For a long time it was thought that this was no more than a decoration. But when these dots were examined under magnification it was discovered that each dot represented a phase of the Moon, and it then became apparent that the pattern was, in fact, a diagram recording the lunar cycle. It was explained that such a device would have been extremely helpful to a hunter in forecasting exactly the time of year his prey, migrating south for the winter, could be expected to arrive. This, to me, was a fascinating example of early man's quite sophisticated method of prognostication. From such practical beginnings arose the science of astrology.

Artefacts of ancient man reveal something of the past to us, but there are occasions when it is as if the past itself impinges upon the fabric of the present. So many incidents have been recorded that it is difficult to select any particular tale, but my favourite is that of the ex-policeman who was working in the ancient tunnel system beneath the city of York, when suddenly, out of one wall appeared a line of Roman soldiers. They moved across the tunnel, apparently a little below the present floor level, and disappeared through the opposite wall! You would be forgiven for concluding that he had suffered an aberration, but he was a man trained to observe accurately, and his description of the dress and equipment tallied with the historical details.

Joan Forman, in her book *The Mask of Time*, gives several well documented accounts of people who have experienced 'time slip'.

She tells of a Mr P. J. Chase of Surrey, who, in 1968, while waiting for a bus, took a short walk down the road, and noticed two straw-thatched cottages, one having the date, 1837, on its wall. He mentioned this to a friend later who argued that he must have been mistaken; there were only two brick houses at that spot. The next evening Mr Chase returned to the same place. He found the houses described by his friend, but the cottages had gone! Enquiries confirmed that two thatched cottages had stood there, but had been demolished many years before.

From extensive researches, Miss Forman was able to make several interesting observations. The type of people most likely to experience 'time slip' are not, as one might suppose, of an over-imaginative nature, but rather the reverse. Quite a high proportion of the contributors to her investigation into the time slip phenomenon were professionals or in the Services, and very few in the arts.

Most observed that the onset of a time slip experience was sudden, followed by some physical effects, like a 'tingling sensation', or, 'a strange feeling of detachment'. Miss Forman notes that several of the sensations mentioned to her are similar to those described by people who have experienced hauntings and other manifestations of the supernatural.

I was particularly interested in her observations because of an experience that occurred while on a visit to the ruined abbey at Castle Acre, Norfolk, England. My son and I had gone ahead of my wife and a friend, climbing the narrow stone stairway to the abbot's private quarters. My son went into the chapel, leaving me standing by a large open fire-place in the ante-chamber. As I stood there, back to the empty hearth, gazing out of the window, I had a sudden impression of standing in a monk's habit, and there was a smell of incense on the air. I was just chiding myself for being too imaginative when my son came through the doorway and asked, 'Can you smell anything, dad?' It turned out that he too could smell incense. The curious thing was that when my wife and friend came up, the smell vanished.

My son and I decided to stay a short while and see if we could track down the smell, having reasoned that it wasn't likely that the incense could have clung to the stone-work after so many centuries. My wife and friend left us and soon we discerned the fragrance of incense again. More sightseers came along and the smell vanished, as before. My son summed up this experience by saying it was rather like bursting a bubble when other people entered, and having the incense escape, to return in 'a wave' when they left. Neither my wife nor friend had smelt anything, and we could find no real explanation for this rather pleasant phenomenon.

From the ample amount of evidence available, it is clear that in some strange way the past can interact with the present. And it is also apparent that we are able to return to the past — without a time-machine! Belief in reincarnation has long been in the Indian tradition, though it took the intriguing case of 'Bridey Murphy' to stimulate the interest of western populations on a wide scale. 'Bridey' was a young American woman whose memory, under hypnosis, regressed beyond birth to nineteenth-century Ireland, where, as a young Irish girl, 'Bridey Murphy', she was able to recall details of her life there in extraordinary detail. Then in Great Britain, came the 'Bloxham Tapes'. These were featured in a documentary film televised by the British Broadcasting Corporation, revealing that Arnall Bloxham, a hypnotherapist, had actually been regressing the memories of his patients for many years. A number of these cases were featured, along with the comments of historians, psychiatrists, and others.

The programme made very clear that details of periods, and language could not have been known to those taking part. For example, one subject, regressed to the life of a gunner's mate aboard a British frigate, HMS *Aggie*, two centuries earlier, used archaic naval slang that no one could understand until explained by naval historians at the National Maritime Museum, Greenwich. This man, Jeffrey Iverson explains in his book (see *Bibliography*), was a soft-spoken Welshman, but the voice and accent he developed under hypnosis was that of a raucous, illiterate, southern Englishman.

Very few of us are likely to undergo hypnosis just for the sake of idle curiosity, and fewer still will ever experience time slip brought about by some apparently extraneous condition of the environment. Yet many people do contact the past, in the world of dreams, and not only in the recalling of past memories. J. W. Dunne, in his book *An Experiment With Time*, explains how his interest first became aroused by a dream. He was staying in a Sussex hotel in 1899, when he dreamt he was having an argument with one of the waiters as to the correct time. He was sure it was half-past-four in the afternoon, though the waiter maintained that it was half-past-four in the middle of the night. Dunne concluded that his watch must have stopped, drew it from his pocket to check, and found that it had stopped, with the hands at four-thirty. He then woke up, full of curiosity, and hunted around for his watch, which was not where he normally left it, by his bedside, but on the chest-of-drawers. Imagine his surprise when he found that it had actually stopped at four-thirty!

Reasoning that it must have stopped the previous afternoon, and that he had forgotten about it, he rewound the watch, though not knowing the correct time, he left the hands as they were. Next morning he went straight to the nearest clock to correct his watch. ''To my absolute amazement,'' he writes, ''I found that the hands had lost only some two or three minutes — about the amount of time which had elapsed between my waking from the dream and rewinding the watch.'' This suggested to him, clearly, that the watch stopped at the moment of the dream. The puzzle was how had he been able to see, in his dream, the actual time.

This experience prompted him, later on, to try a simple experiment. Lying half awake one morning, and too lazy to get up and look at his watch, he tried visualizing it in 'clairvoyant fashion'. He then describes what he saw: ''The vision I saw was binocular, upright, poised in space about a foot from my nose, illumined by ordinary daylight, and encircled by a thick, whitish mist . . .'' Having decided that the hands pointed to about two-and-a-half minutes past eight, he then reached out under the mosquito curtains for his watch (he was in Italy at the time), and found that it actually was two-and-a-half minutes past eight!

A year or two later he dreamt of a trek from South Africa to the Nile, and woke to find the headlines in his daily paper read: 'The Cape To Cairo'. Details of this trans-continental journey were remarkably similar to those of his dream. Over a period of time he had several precognitive dreams and these stimulated his interest in the nature of time. I should point out to you that such dreams often occur after the actual event, but before the news of them arrives. Thus, although it is as if the unconscious mind is receiving an impression of an actual occurrence after it has taken place, and is therefore picking up images from the past, the dream is precognitive in that it anticipates the receipt of the information.

A friend of mine has had similar dream experiences for many years. At one time she thought it was quite abnormal, and suffered a great deal of needless anxiety. A study of her birth-chart revealed tendencies akin to those one might expect to find in the psychological make-up of individuals claiming to have clairvoyant gifts. For example, her chart showed a high degree of receptivity, with quick mental response coupled to a sector of the chart traditionally associated with prophecy, but which we now consider as referring to the wider function of the intellect in its capacity for visualization. In one dream she told me of how she felt ''the ground tremble beneath my feet once, then violent trembling — seeing the ground crack, buildings crumble — white buildings — seeing people in black buried beneath white rubble. I saw my cactus being crushed — the cactus I brought back from Italy the year before.'' Three days after this dream she read about the Italian earthquake disaster of November 1980.

The eminent philosopher, Bertrand Russell, was of the opinion that the memory works backwards and not forwards. Certainly, in the light of what we now know concerning the nature of the unconscious mind, it is possible to regress it, and not only in sleep or hypnotic trance. Scientists have found, for example, that certain parts of the brain, under stimulus from an electrode, can be made to play back details of long forgotten memories with the clarity of a video-tape. As you will have realized, an enquiry into the nature of time is really an investigation into mankind, and the awareness we have of the environment in which we exist. However, let us now move on to the next section.

Present

Memory, of course, is essential for establishing our perspective in time. Until about age two, children have difficulty in remembering where they left their toys a few hours previously. By age three they can usually recall what happened yesterday, and after a few more years of development the idea of days and months passing is finally grasped. This acquired sense of time duration can, however, be easily disturbed. For example, under drugs like cannabis, the individual may think that a long period has elapsed, although only a few moments have gone by.

Due to minor differences in our physiological make-up, we may function either a little more quickly or slowly than someone else. Because of this it is probable that our impression of time passing also differs fractionally, although, it has been found that under hypnosis people exhibit a surprising accuracy for estimating time. In part, this is probably due to our biological clocks. Apparently, there are groups of cells that fluctuate at regular intervals, and there is an area in the brain producing an alpha-rhythm of approximately 10 oscillations per second.

There are other rhythms or cycles, of course, although only three have achieved any sort of prominence. I refer to the biorhythms. These have gained considerable popularity since the seventies although they were first observed many years before. There is a 23-day physical cycle, and a 28-day emotional cycle. These were first found by Dr Wilhelm Fleiss, a medical specialist, in collaboration with psychologist Dr Hermann Swoboda. They were both interested in cycles of various kinds, and much of their work was done around the turn of the century. The third cycle, of 33 days, was observed by teacher and engineer, Alfred Teltscher, in the twenties. He noticed that learning ability appeared to have a low and a peak, each with an interval of just over a month. Eventually, these three biorhythms became so popular that tables for their calculation were published, a plastic calculator was produced, and then the calculations were introduced as an extra function on some of the electronic pocket calculators.

It is of interest to note that the 28-day emotional cycle is almost the same length as the 28½-day lunar and female cycle, and the 33-day intellectual cycle is close to being the same period as a calendar month — the approximate time it takes the Sun to move through each of the twelve signs of the zodiac. However, although the pattern of human biological rhythms may well have been established or influenced by the regular cycles of the Sun and Moon at the dawn of the world, there is no connection between the three biorhythms and astrological inferences.

From what we have seen so far it is obvious that the mind has a propensity to scan back and forth in time, even if we are not always aware of this. After studying the dreams of many people, Dunne found ''that the images which relate indisputably to the near-by future are about equal in number to those which pertain *similarly indisputably* to the near-by past.''

Dunne's book, published in 1925, was followed some nine years later, in America, by the now famous researches of Dr Joseph Rhine. Dr Rhine was the first person to submit para-normal states of mind to scientific investigation. It was he who first used the term 'extra-sensory perception' or ESP as it is popularly known. His experiment was to have someone 'transmit' a thought image to a subject, using a pack of cards, each bearing a simple figure, such as a circle, a square, a cross, and so on. It was found that some subjects were much better at receiving than others, and their scores for correctly deducing which card had been turned up were consistently high; well beyond that of chance. Distance appeared to make little difference to the results, though what proved to be particularly remarkable was when it was discovered that one able subject was perceiving, not the card that was being 'transmitted', but the one that had yet to be turned up by the sender, and therefore unknown. This prompted Dr Rhine to develop the experiment by having the pack shuffled, and then asking his subjects to guess the order of cards before they were actually seen. The results were again above that of chance.

This carefully conducted investigation would seem to confirm Dunne's conclusion from dream experiences that it is possible for us to 'see' "images which relate indisputably to the near-by future." In Einstein's Law of Relativity there is no clear distinction between past, present, and future. From which it could be reasoned that past and future co-exist, and from such views has arisen the concept of a 'block universe'. The problem is that there are a great many concepts of time, or 'time models' as they are often called.

Dunne tried to find a scientific explanation, and his book contains many references to the theories of academics. From these he formulated his own model which he termed, 'Serial Time'. In this he postulated ". . . a single multi-dimensional field of presentation in absolute motion, travelling over a fixed substratum of objective elements extending in all directions of Time."

This hypothesis was not without its difficulties for it necessitated a continuing sequence of "Time-travelling fields of presentation . . .", each contained within another larger field, rather like those wooden, Russian dolls, ". . . the larger field covering events which are 'past' and 'future', as well as 'present', to the smaller field." He goes on to propose that "The serialism of the fields of presentation involves the existence of a serial observer . . ." But I think that it is sufficient just to convey to you an impression of what is involved in this type of intellectualizing.

However, it is one thing to endeavour to explain time with the aid of highly abstruse models, but it still leaves us wondering about the nature of the mind itself, in its apparent ability to range through time. Some facts are clear. Dr Edward de Bono has observed: "The mind functions to create patterns out of its surroundings." (See *Bibliography*). We know that at the most basic level the mind functions in a numerical way. The brain responds to the biological oscillations and inherent rhythms of the life-force, converting these pulses into, first unconscious, then conscious images. Number is the outcome of these oscillations and rhythms.

As Marie-Louise von Franz observes (see *Bibliography*), "When energy manifests itself in either psychic or physical dimensions, it is always 'numerically' structured, e.g., as 'waves' or as (psychic) rhythm. Natural numbers appear to represent the typical, universally recurring, common motion patterns of both psychic *and* physical energy.'' And she goes on to observe: "The existence of such numerical nature constants in the outer world, on the one hand, and in the preconscious psyche, on the other (e.g., in the quaternary structures of the 'psychic centre', the triadic structure of dynamic processes, the dualistic structure of threshold phenomena, and so forth) is probably what finally makes all conscious knowledge of nature possible.''

I believe this observation of an eminent scientist and co-worker of Carl Jung will provide you with some idea of the mental processes, as they derive from the physiological and organic structures in the form of energy, but you may not be familiar with her reference to numerical values. I will try to explain. 'Quaternary' relates, of course, to four, a number which, in numerology would be said to impart a strong-willed, serious quality, with an underlying dynamism that can be utilized both constructively and destructively. (Mary Anderson, *The Secret Power Of Numbers*.)

If we take Dr von Franz's description, then four is ''. . . The model of wholeness in all relatively closed structures of human consciousness and in the body.'' In the outer world we find 'four' occurring throughout the history of mankind in one form or another. In geometrical figures its value is found in the square and the cross. A well-built house is said to stand 'four-square'. The cross, in Christianity, is one of the most powerful symbols, depicting as it does, both the positive and negative principles, i.e. the destruction in sacrifice, yet eternal in that we, as human beings, can identify with the structure because it is inherent as a universal principle, and therefore cannot be erased.

This is why, as a 'psychic centre', four, along with three, recur persistently throughout legend and religion. 'Triadic' refers to the qualitative principle of three. Dr von Franz attributes to it a quality pertaining to 'dynamic processes'. In numerology it is said to relate to creative self-expression, with a buoyant and optimistic outlook. It has about it a sense of balanced growth with, therefore, the potential to preserve existing structures. As you will know, the most common beat in music is three-four time. Preservation, in the mystical sense, is also apparent in the Holy Trinity of Christianity.

''Dualistic structures of threshold phenomena . . .'' Well, here, Dr von Franz is speaking as a psychologist. 'Duality' obviously relates to two. This number she describes elsewhere in her book as ". . . rhythm by which symmetries and observables are engendered.'' If we reason that 'one' is the monad principle of 'I', or Godhead, or 'Oneness', self-existent until a second principle is introduced, then, as soon as a second object or entity is taken into consideration, a duality exists, and this will set up an oscillation between the two, hence the reference to rhythm.

This basic rhythm may be seen in the interplay between dark and light, male and female, yin-yang, and so on. If 'one' exists in isolation it cannot know itself, and having nothing to relate to, cannot form a sense of perspective or dimension. But when a second principle (two) is present, then observation becomes possible, as well as a sense of symmetry. Numerologically, two is said to be synonymous with female qualities, adaptability, and understanding or intuitive, emotional response.

'Threshold phenomena'. Here, Dr von Franz is referring to the threshold of the unconscious. In the analysis of dreams — as part of psychoanalysis for therapeutic purposes — it has been found that when a person dreams of a pair of anything, or alternatively of being accompanied by a shadowy, vaguely familiar figure (because it is actually the 'shadow' self), thus creating a duality, it usually heralds a dream-state that takes one deeper into the unconscious, or the collective unconscious — which is the lair of all those primeval images (archetypal) referred to earlier.

It was Carl Jung who first realized that the archetypal images — products of the unconscious, both of a personal and universal quality — had a numerical foundation. Though, of course, the qualitative principle of number has been recognized since the earliest times. To give you a brief example: in astrology the Sun is the central, integrating factor, the giver of life and light. To it is attributed the number 'one'. It is considered as having a masculine principle, and is traditionally related to conscious awareness and intellect. The Moon, reflecting the Sun's light upon the earth at night, and whose monthly cycle marks the ebb and flow of the tides, (and life, for it is a fact that there are more births at the time of the full moon!) correlates with two, the female principle, the unconscious, and the flux of emotional responses. Obviously, both the astrological and numerical references are but symbols of the unseen properties, vortices or eddies in the life-force, having a universal nature though experienced differently in the psyche of every individual, depending upon sex, culture, and so on.

If one takes the planetary potential for any moment and place in time, the symbolism will *always* be appropriate to the nature of experiences that may happen to occur, and can be expressed in terms relevant to the type of emotional and psychological responses most likely to be evinced.

For example, if we take the British European Airways Trident crash, a major air disaster, in June 1972, the cosmogram (a modern form of horoscope) read-out produces: "Journey of short duration." (The aircraft crashed just after take-off.) "Loss of power. Danger — to face overwhelming force without power. Failures caused through wrong arrangements or instructions, through premature action. . . . Crisis — sudden ruin through misuse of power. Depression. Separations. Termination of associations." And more of the same nature. These interpretations of planetary patterns reflect almost exactly the actual conditions, although please note, they do not predict any specific event. And let me hasten to emphasize that they are not my wording but taken from a standard handbook of cosmobiology by Reinhold Ebertin. (See *Bibliography*.)

Just to give you a comparison, here is part of the read-out for cosmograms at the time of the London and Liverpool (Toxteth) youth riots of April and July 1981: "Acts of sudden violence. Sudden difficulties or separations in communities of people. Violence in contact with others. Self destroying energy — violence — frustrations." And so on. Again, not my words, but taken from the handbook. You will see that words like 'violence' are repeated. When different combinations of planets produce similar types of behavioural response pictures, the chances of an event of similar nature actually coming into manifestation are greatly increased.

It could be argued, of course, that these young people were only reacting to the frustrations of their environments and the climate produced by the world-wide recession. True, but why in exactly the way they did? Well, if we take the mean average age to be about 17 years — I have no way of verifying this, but also in 1981 a youth of 17 years fired a blank shot at our beloved Queen — this takes us back to a birth year of 1964. During this year some of the major planetary patterns gave: "Plans unreasonable beyond measure. Instability and pessimism. One-sided principles, obstinacy. The stage of losing one's inner balance jointly with others. Feelings of inferiority."

Seen as birth-chart (horoscope) 'influences', these major patterns, through the year, would have stamped their qualities upon the personalities of some proportion of the population.

Obviously, and fortunately for society as a whole, not every individual is going to express these qualities in a negative way. Even so, these are underlying tendencies inherent in the generation now reaching adulthood, and as such should be observed with due care, especially in the international context.

Future

If you had asked me, in 1964, to 'predict' the events in Britain for 1981, I would have told you — in common with any responsible astrologer — that it is impossible. Why? Because we do not make predictions. Forecast tendencies, certainly, but that is quite a different matter, in line with what a skilled accountant does when he extrapolates the past and present financial activities of his company in order to forecast the likely sales turnover and profits for the year ahead. Likewise, the weathermen do not attempt to predict the weather, they only make forecasts as to the likely outcome of weather patterns.

What I could have done for you, in 1964, would have been to assess the patterns for 1981, either in a general chart, or as relating to the birth-chart of a child born during 1964. This ability to evaluate the likely trends for any given period, up to around the year 2000, is made possible by virtue of the fact that astronomical tables for the planetary position are readily available.

As you may have realized, in referring to forecasting by means of observable and measurable factors, i.e. the regular cycles of the planets, I am discussing a casual factor. Scientists are just beginning to realize that there is a definite link between the cosmic play and human behaviour. But we have also seen that the mind appears to have an extraordinary ability to reach through space and time. Parapsychologists might be able to throw a little light upon this phenomenon, though for the moment, all I can do is present my own view, perhaps rather metaphysical, though based upon the facts as we understand them at present.

The use of Tarot cards, sticks or coins for the I Ching, or any other system of divination, does no more than tap the springs of the unconscious. For example, the few times I have tried the I Ching I have always found that the hexagrams (numerical patterns) simply reveal what I recognized as having been below the level of consciousness, anyway. The gipsy fortune-teller, gazing into her crystal ball, first falls into a sleep-like state. What she sees is the projection of unconscious images, apparently in the crystal, although actually upon the inner-eye, just as in a dream.

These images are produced by a perfectly natural phenomenon, though we usually grow out of it. I refer to the common childhood experience of half-waking from a vivid dream and still being able to see the dream action, apparently on the wall or ceiling of our bedroom. Thus, the seer, in whatever method is used, is actually attempting to contact the personal and collective unconscious layers of the mind. ESP plays a part in this, because there is obviously some interplay below the level of consciousness, between the seer and consultee.

The images, as we have already seen, can be of a profound and universal nature, shared, as Carl Jung observes, by all peoples in all times. Books on fortune-telling by dream interpretation, or how to read the crystal ball, or Tarot cards, and so on, all have the archetypal images as a common denominator. And methods of prognostication that rely upon the casting of objects, for example, coins, bones, runes, sand, and so on, in an apparently random fashion, are tapping directly into the fundamental area of number and geometric forms.

It is interesting to note Dr von Franz's comments about the hexagram of the I Ching. Referring to the eight possible arrangements resulting from combinations of triple lines, she writes, "One cannot escape the impression that these numerical combinations are introspective representations of fundamental processes in a psychophysical nature; . . ." She goes on to refer to the numerical construction of the DNA molecule, which has four constituents at its base, combined into three. Thus, "From the four bases sixty-four different triplets come into being . . . In these genetic findings we are confronted with an exchange of 'information' in living cells that corresponds exactly to the structure of the I Ching hexagrams."

When the cards, coins, sticks, tea leaves, and so forth, fall into an apparently random pattern or sequence, we are inclined to think that it is pure chance, but is this so? It is now thought that impulses from the unconscious level of the mind may well be producing imperceptible muscular activity, so that our movements are stimulated by environmental conditions, perhaps rather more than we realize. A good example of this can be found in the use of the divining rod or pendulum — instruments used to find water, metals, and so on. At one time it was thought that either the rod or its user had 'magical' properties. More likely is the possibility that the instrument used is simply magnifying a minute tremor in the body of the operator.

It is well known that practitioners of the divining or dowsing art need to be in the right frame of mind; not distracted by too many external influences or disturbances. It is evident that, initially, the subconscious level of the mind is somehow responding to a microscopic alteration in certain 'wave' lengths, or 'vibrations'. This is not really surprising when we consider that subtle alterations of mood and emotion can be brought about by sound and light waves, i.e. in music and paintings.

Even in so broad and so brief a review as this, it will be obvious to you that if there are any secrets about time they are integral with the nature of man and his evolution. And the nearest we can come to an understanding of time, certainly in the context of precognition, is in the observation of the mind of man. Particularly the subconscious, which is the repository of the archetypes and the receptor of psychic energy rhythms (emotional responses), which gradually filter up into consciousness.

That it seems possible to forecast events by direct utilization of preconscious images was dramatically illustrated by Dr Carl Jung, although I doubt whether he intended to actually prophesy. Long before the Great War of 1914, in his work as a psychiatrist, he observed in the dream material of many patients, images of a collective and disquieting nature. So many people having the same sort of dream symbolism alerted his suspicions, and he eventually realized that their portent was social or national rather than individual.

Again, during his notable lectures at the Tavistock Clinic in London, in 1935, he once more voiced his concern. "Who would have thought in 1900 that it would be possible thirty years later for such things to happen in Germany as are happening today? Would you have believed that a whole nation of highly intelligent and cultivated people could be seized by the fascinating power of an archetype? I saw it coming, and I can understand it because I know the power of the collective unconscious. But on the surface it looks simply incredible." (*Analytical Psychology*). He was, of course, referring to the growing Hitler movement.

Some twelve years after the Second World War, Jung again expressed his concern in a short but memorable work, *The Undiscovered Self*, which starts off with the question, "What will the future bring?" and which he then proceeds to answer with a frighteningly accurate description of how the power of the collective in the form of the State — he was referring to the USSR — destroys the integrity of individuals. He might have written this book in 1982 instead of 1958, i.e. when the book was first published.

However, the point is that if some 'fortune-teller' or clairvoyant had claimed to have 'seen' the advent of the First and Second World Wars they would probably have been acclaimed for their marvellous powers of prediction. Let us trust, incidentally, that Jung's concern for the latter part of the second millennium is not proved justified. With regard to the astrological view, I have already made reference to certain trends, though I should explain that my own work, primarily, is concerned with individuals rather than nations, which is the province of the mundane or political astrologer.

2. DO WE HAVE FREE-WILL?

In the Introduction I referred to a Professor of Sociology I had watched taking part in a television chat-show on astrology and clairvoyance, and how agitated he appeared to become over the whole question of predicting a person's future. (I think you will understand by now that the serious astrologer never claims to 'predict' an actual event). He reasoned, quite rightly, that such an act takes away a person's freedom of choice, but he was so insistent about the importance of preserving free-will that this point rather overshadowed the debate. The amusing thing about his doing this was that while he vigorously denied the credibility of astrology, and appeared to offer proof as to why it didn't work, one was then led to wonder why he felt the need to be so emphatic about its apparent dangers! If astrology was the nonsense he suggested, why the concern?

Mind you, this somewhat contradictory attitude on the part of academics is not uncommon. In 1978, for example, a group of American scientists, calling themselves the Committee for the Scientific Investigation of Claims of the Paranormal, was accused of covering up and even distorting solid, statistical evidence which demonstrated clearly the effect of planets upon human behaviour. (*Phenomena,* vol. 2.2, Mar-Apr 78.) Of course, there is a reason why apparently rational and intelligent people should act in such an illogical manner. The short answer is, fear. Fear of the unknown, and fear of anything that seems to threaten the structures of too rigid an ego. In my experience, scientists of vision and capability have little difficulty in accepting the principles of astrology with an open mind, while those of a somewhat closed temperament are either apathetic or negatively antagonistic.

Exactly the same thing applies whenever astrology is drawn into religious discussion. There are those who vehemently claim that the practice of anything of a predictive nature is 'wicked', or against the teachings of the Bible. They conveniently overlook the fact that prophecy abounds in the Holy Book, and that much of the symbolism employed is astrological, and numerological. For example, before the invention of the telescope, there were only seven heavenly bodies that could be seen with the naked eye: Sun, Moon, Mercury, Venus, Mars, Jupiter, and as far as Saturn. This planet marked the limits of man's known universe. Thus, seven became established in the mystical and mythological symbology of the time. Indeed, it is a number that has traditionally been related to healing and the priesthood, and we find seven referred to quite often in the Bible.

The miracle of the five loaves and two fishes is particularly interesting because there appears to be a close parallel to both astrological and numerological symbolism. Early Christians used the mark of a fish for their insignia, and the sign of Pisces, comprising two fishes, is opposite in the Zodiac to Virgo, the Virgin, who is often depicted as carrying a sheaf of wheat. And incidentally, the astronomical phenomenon, the precession of the equinoxes, gave rise to the 'Age of Pisces' at approximately the time of Christ, just as now, in our scientific and technocratic society, we are moving into the 'Age of Aquarius.'

However, to return to the miracle of the loaves and fishes. The fragments of bread and fishes were gathered into *twelve* baskets. (The same number as the signs of the Zodiac.) And five plus two equal seven. Coincidence or not, the use of astrological symbolism in the recounting of this event by St Mark, whether consciously or unconsciously, surely enhances the story, imparting to it a spiritual and cosmic quality that would certainly have reached to the heart of a people who were, perhaps, more in tune with the natural world and universe than urbanized, modern man.

It is frequently those who are blatantly sectarian in their beliefs, and therefore the most insecure, who clamour against the 'wickedness' of occult subjects. On the other hand, the more enlightened and exalted are religious representatives, the easier it is to converse with them in a rational manner. I have enjoyed pleasant discussions on the moral implications of astrology with dignitaries of the Church of England and the Roman Catholic faith. It is fairly well understood, for example, that St Augustine, in philosophical as well as religious terms, recognised the infinite as a constant, and observed (*De Civitate Dei*), that "time and motion must be extremely carefully distinguished. In particular, time must not be correlated with the motion of the heavenly bodies." He turned to the soul and the spiritual rather than to physical concepts. And, of course, he was correct in taking this view. It is completely wrong for anyone, whether devoutly religious or not, to be so ensnared by the overweening belief in 'the stars' that they cannot make a move without first checking the position of the planets.

On the other hand, St Augustine did not entirely ignore the likelihood of there being a planetary influence. As St Thomas Aquinas makes clear: "Now the disposition of the human body is subject to the heavenly movements. For Augustine says (*De Civ. Dei,* v.6.) that 'it is not altogether absurd to ascribe the mere differences between bodies to the influence of the stars'." Aquinas goes on to note that (*Summa Contra Gentiles*), "Consequently the heavenly bodies co-operate indirectly to the goodness of our intelligence; and thus, even as physicians are able to judge of a man's intelligence from his bodily temperament, as a proximate disposition thereto, so too can an astrologer, from the heavenly movements, as being a remote cause of his disposition . . ."

From such writings it is perfectly clear that eminent theologians have been prepared to acknowledge astrological concepts. Indeed, it would have been foolish of them to entirely ignore such things, for, as Jung says in his *Analytical Psychology,* there is an "unconscious astrology which is in our bones, though we are unaware of it." A good example of this is to be found in the way our churches are oriented, with the chancel end due east. Thus, the congregation in the nave or body of the church not only faces the altar, but also towards the rising Sun.

In this respect there is a curious similarity between the ground-plan of a church and the structure of the horoscope wheel with its twelve spokes radiating from the centre, and its orientation, which is established by the eastern horizon point, or 'Ascendant', as we call it. The interpretation of this point, in astrology, is of fundamental importance, even more so than the well-known Sun-sign. As Jung observes, "The East is not a Tibetan monastery . . . It is from the depths of our own psychic life." (*Modern Man In Search of a Soul*).

It is of interest, too, to note that 'chancel' means a lattice or screen of laths. We might visualize, therefore, the chancel, with its altar, as being the place where the clergy commune with, and call upon the 'power' of God. It also serves as a screen or filter to diffuse, as it were, God's power, to the lesser mortals in the congregation.

The nave, in which the congregation sits, also means, in its earlier derivation, the central block or hub of a wheel which holds the spokes. The 'spokes' of a horoscope are the twelve cusp lines which separate the various sectors of life experience for each individual. There is, incidentally, a design of the Zodiac wheel set into the floor in front of the altar of one of the university chapels in the ancient city of Oxford. Medical students of the Middle Ages were expected to have a working knowledge of the anatomical and physiological correlations with the planets.

Thinking back to the attitude of the professor in that television show, and his main theme, which was the loss of free-will incurred by the individuals who have their fortunes told, I could not help but reflect upon the crass arrogance of people like him, for they seem to lose sight of the fact that free-will is, at best, rather a delusive thing.

In psychological terms, our consciousness is akin to the tip of an iceberg, and our tiny egos are but a fraction of that! Residing below whatever sense of self-awareness we may have, and it is really precious little, there is that vast world of the subconscious, with its layers of personal unconscious material interwoven into the deeper fabric of the collective unconscious, in which the genetic memory patterns vie with the cosmic impresses.

If you believe that your actions are completely self-determined, think again. Fortunately, only those of small imagination and inflated egos fall into the trap of self-delusion, and it is well to recall that Christianity, like most great religions, teaches humility. This is a sure safeguard against loss of wholeness (holiness) that results when the small 'I' tries to grow away from the total personality, or psyche.

Of course, this is not to deny the individual's freedom of choice, and there is a clear difference, for example, in an astrologer indicating possible trends and tendencies, and, say, the gipsy fortune-teller's classic pronouncement that, "You will meet a tall, dark, handsome stranger!" Such a prediction might just prove to be true, and indeed, in the light of what we have already seen, it could be within the realms of possibility, but this type of prediction assumes a rather too rigid and fatalistic view, and does nothing towards enhancing the recipient's quality of life, or development as an individual.

This tenuous thing we call individuality, personality, soul or psyche, exists, obviously, in time and space. Phenomena, like time slip, precognitive dreams, various methods of divination or prognosticating, and so on, clearly indicate to us that there must be something more to the human mind than just an awareness of what is going on in the immediate environment. Researches, such as the controlled studies of Dr Rhine, add their scientific weight to the overwhelming evidence in support of that mysterious 'something'. Even the causally oriented scientists can no longer refute the fact that not everything can be accounted for by the law of causality.

Physicists were at a loss to explain the half-life of radioactive decay. As Sir James Jeans observed, "Radioactive break-up appeared to be an effect without a cause, and suggested that the ultimate laws of nature were not even causal." (*Physics & Philosophy*, Cambridge 1942.) Since then the frontiers of science have been extended a great deal, and the lack of an adequate explanation for certain events, as in the behaviour of particles, or animals, is now even more acutely felt, and efforts to counter this have been attempted. For example, Rupert Sheldrake, aware of the current theoretical limitations in the areas of genetics and molecular biology, hypothesizes a non-energy field operating independently of time and space, through 'morphic resonance'. Such a concept, he hopes, will help to explain the results of experiments with animals that cannot be accounted for by the usual, casual principles. (*New Scientist*, 18 June, 1981.)

A concept like 'morphic resonance', which is, literally, a form-like vibration, is, it seems to me, very close to Carl Jung's hypothesis of 'synchronicity'. (I return to Jung constantly because he is the only reliable authority when it comes to any observation of the world beyond consciousness.) During his study of dream images he became intrigued by the precognitive faculty and the possible relationship with the concept of the soul, or psyche. In this respect, he had observed over many years, through dream analyses, the "presence of a formal factor in nature." That is to say, a consistent theme in many of his patients' dreams which seemed to be a ". . . meaningful coincidence of an absolutely natural product with a human idea apparently independent of it."

To give some brief examples: One patient told Jung of a dream in which he was walking in mountainous country and came across a little brown man, the same colour as the rock, hollowing out a cave. In the cave was a cluster of columns, each having a dark brown human head. The dreamer's impression was that the rock was at least half-a-million years old.

In another dream, a lady patient described discovering a large sand-pit containing rubbish, in a garden. Among the layers of rubbish were thin, slaty plates of green serpentine. One of them had black squares on it, arranged concentrically, and apparently ingrained in the stone. In a similar dream to the first, another male patient finds himself walking in a wild mountain region, and upon loosening slabs of rock, he finds, to his amazement, human heads in low relief.

Dreams of this type seemed to Jung to suppose a pre-existent psyche which organizes matter. As you will appreciate, I'm sure, it is only possible to convey to you a superficial impression of an idea that raises all sorts of philosophical conjectures, but it would mean digressing too far from the main theme of this book to pursue all of Jung's more abstract thoughts.

However, one area that Jung took into consideration is graphic enough to be of interest, and it is relevant to our question concerning free-will because it refers directly to the sense of individuality, and the belief that there is a part of us, call it soul, synchronous phenomenon, morphic resonance, or what you will, that can and does exist beyond space and time. A patient told Jung that she almost died while in hospital, and at the critical moment, physically unconscious, experienced herself looking down upon her own body in bed, and at the nurse and doctor. The account was of particular interest to me because a friend of mine had almost exactly the same type of 'out-of-the-body experience'. She apparently died while on the operating table, and for some time was able to view the scene from ceiling level, in one corner of the operating theatre. And, just like Jung's patient, she was able to describe in detail all that occurred, once she regained consciousness.

As uncanny as they appear to be, these out-of-the-body experiences are so widely known and so well recorded as to be a virtually established fact. They give rise to the fascinating question of whether there is life after death, but the reason for referring to this particular phenomenon here is because it too seems to confirm ''a knowledge not mediated by the sense organs . . . Such a form of existence can only be transcendental, since, as the knowledge of the future or spatially distant events shows, it is contained in a psychically relative space and time, that is to say in an irrepresentable space-time continuum.'' In observations like this, as well as in his concept of an 'absolute knowledge' Jung attempted to define what he termed 'synchronistic phenomena'.

Evidently, there is within the nature of human beings a capability of extension beyond the physical limits, and it is much the same whether you call it astral body, soul or psyche. And it seems evident, too, that the faculty of ESP, clairvoyance or precognition, all operate at this same level. Incidentally, it is of interest to note that in practically all documented out-of-the-body experiences, the individuals concerned were all aware of floating upwards, sometimes into bright light. This curiously parallels the evidence gleaned from observing the archetypal images employed in literature, as referred to earlier.

It seems to me that such universal indications as these vividly confirm the rightness of religious fundamentals. It is in the very nature of man to reach towards heaven, to pray to a God above, to move from darkness into light. In this sense then, it is fitting to reach forward and, metaphorically at least, upwards, for the opposite direction must obviously be negative and retrogressive!

Science, of necessity, has developed along materialistic lines. Causality is its doctrine because the establishment of observable, measurable facts demands a rigid interpretation of whatever is under examination. And everything that exists must have a concrete explanation, must be given its rational beginning and its inevitable end. Religion, with its concepts of spirituality and faith, is the other side of the coin. No matter what the objections of some well-meaning though poorly informed people may be, there is obviously a greater affinity between occult subjects with their acausal and irrepresentable nature, and religious beliefs, than there is to the material sciences.

Clearly, when we speak of the desire to preserve free-will, and uphold moral and spiritual values by avoiding anything that might be considered too fatalistic, it is not always the subject — indeed, I would go so far as to say that it is never the subject — that is at fault, but the manner in which it is utilized. I remember reading a report of a German lady who went to an astrologer, and as a result of what she was told, at once took herself off to the nearest lake, and drowned herself! Of course, the practice of astrology was blamed. Yet, obviously, it was the interpretation of the astrologer, and the way in which it had been presented.

Some years ago I received a letter from a psychiatrist friend concerning a patient who had come to him for treatment. Part of the reason for her 'break-down' had apparently been one of those cut-price horoscope 'readings' that are frequently offered by women's magazines. I examined this and found that the commercial astrologer who had attempted to interpret her horoscope had quite overlooked certain basic personality tendencies that this lady had, and which were clearly evident as chart (horoscope) features, and had obviously not seen the implication of the current movements of the planetary bodies to her chart, which very clearly indicated a critical, depressive phase. The way in which the reading had been worded was so devoid of insight and understanding that it was no wonder that it virtually precipitated an emotional episode.

If there is any question of moral issues being involved in 'telling the future' it is, to my mind, not the means but the manner of its application that should be under dispute. If human beings can be thoughtless at times, can you imagine what the results will be when commercial enterprises decide to employ computers in fortune-telling! Devoid of any ability to observe each person as a unique being, a computer cannot take into account the essence or soul of the individual, however cleverly it may have been programmed. And yet, I believe that in some countries astro-readings by computer are already available. But whether a horoscope is interpreted by a human being or a machine, if it is as the outcome of commercialism rather than of personal service to the individual, it becomes a piece of mass-production without any capacity to reflect upon either the psyche or the environment, and therefore degrades, for it reduces the concept of personality to a mere unit value, and a much limited one at that.

In the field of astrology, at least, there is a recognized distinction between the serious, qualified practitioner, and the commercial purveyor of predictions. Speaking from my own experience as a senior tutor and examiner for the Mayo School of Astrology, students of astrology, these days, are not only taught the basic techniques of the subject but are also introduced to the procedures of counselling, and the role of psychology (particularly that of Jung), in the modern concept of analytical astrology. Moreover, students taking examinations for diplomas are required to sign a Code of Ethics. This, in fact, has been a standard requirement in Britain for the last thirty years or so. In other words, there already exists responsible bodies of astrologers who are ever mindful of the social and ethical implications that are inherent in astrological practice.

Until now I have presented astrology in something of a defensive light, so before we leave the question of fate and free-will, and the moral problems that appear to be raised by the predictive arts and sciences, it might be as well if we consider the positive and constructive results that can be achieved through the proper application of astrological technique. It will be clearly evident to you from the references to the many ways in which the mind extends in time and space, that when we presume to acquire knowledge of the future, by whatever means, we are inevitably involving ourselves directly with the human condition, and that precious something just beyond the grasp of conscious perception. When Jung's patients had completed a course of psycho-therapy he found they often continued to explore their inner selves with the help of dream analysis, to which he had introduced them. The process of self-discovery is the natural expression of our desire to become more than we are. That is to say, to achieve fulfilment, or 'realization', or, to become 'one with God'.

It is just this instinctive and intuitive urge for self-realization that stands in danger of being over-shadowed by today's group oriented society. Be it the siren-clamour of the technocratic age, the ability to manipulate the minds of the mass through the 'media', or the stultifying materialism of State conditioning that usurps the individual's responsibility to his or her self, it remains an essential part of the continuous development of human beings to ever seek for self-knowledge.

It is a sad fact that the Church, in the Western world at least, seems to have lost its understanding of the spiritual needs of society, and appears to spend an increasing amount of time and energy in politicizing. Yet, people always feel when there is an imbalance between the conscious and the unconscious, i.e. the earthly and the spiritual, and instinctively seek to correct it. That is why, in recent years, there has been a resurgence of interest in occult subjects.

Astrology, because of its ability to reveal, not only the framework of personality but also the intricate patterns of potential within, stands unique as a system for determining inner truths. And it bestrides the pathway of civilization as it winds from our primitive past, like a portal to future enlightenment.

The importance of our instinctive search for self-knowledge should not be underestimated. Everyone who becomes acutely aware of their inadequacies when faced with the overwhelming pressures of today's society, will begin to question themselves, will want to know the reason why they should feel as they do, and may question the reason for their very existence.

Futile attempts to escape from reality, as in drug taking and the like, do not, of course, answer our needs. Shifting the blame for our own weaknesses upon others only brings about alienation and division. Yet, if we are only able to examine ourselves and our inner motivations, as under a microscope, and if we are willing to accept what we find, then, as Jung points out in *The Undiscovered Self*, "... he will not only discover some important truths about himself, but will also have gained a psychological advantage ... and taken the first step towards the foundation of his consciousness, that is, towards the unconscious, the only accessible source of religious experience." Of course, Jung explains that the unconscious is not identified with God, but only that religious experience seems to flow from it.

I think you will now understand what I meant about the manner in which astrology is applied. It can be, and often is used as a divining medium — I'll be explaining some of the methods to you in Chapter 4 — but, just like classical music compared with 'pop', when utilized with professional discipline, insight and understanding, it has the ability to release the potentials of the personality and lift the spirit to fresh heights. Albeit, one cannot pretend that the path to self-knowledge is an easy one, whatever the means taken to pursue it, and neither, for that matter, is the role of the analytical astrologer consultant, who requires an immense amount of dedication.

3. THE HOROSCOPE AND SPACE-TIME

In October 1981, it was reported that American marine archaeologists had discovered an anchor-stone from which they were able to establish that the arrival of Chinese ships to the shores of California was at least 2,000 years before Columbus. We might ask how this remarkable feat of navigation was accomplished? One thing we know for certain is that the Chinese did have compasses. However, what is even more fascinating is that before they invented the compass its principle was originally used for divinatory purposes. There were divining boards marked with the cardinal points (North, South, East, and West), and the circle of the earth (Yin), above which was a rotating plate of the heavens (Yang). To answer questions the two boards were spun in opposite directions.

By the sixteenth century, Chinese navigators were using portable compasses combined with a sundial, and the means for adjusting it to the latitude they happened to be sailing on (beautifully made instruments are still in existence — *v*. Needham, *Science and Civilization in China*, vol. 3.) Once the system of co-ordinates (latitude and longitude) was universally established, mankind was well on the way to circumnavigation of the world.

Incidentally, sundials, as a means for telling the time, have, of course, been a familiar sight for many centuries. They were placed on the south side of churches to mark the time for prayer, and can often be seen today. One of the oldest of these sun clocks can be found on the wall of the Saxon Church at Corhampton, Hampshire, not very far from where I live. It must be at least a thousand years old.

The system of longitudinal lines section the globe from north to south pole, rather like the segments of an orange. The circle of the equator is divided into 360 degrees, as too is the ecliptic (apparent path of the Sun). Thus, the traveller upon the surface of the world and the astronomer peering into the star-lit sky, have a means for measuring and recording positions in space. With the advance from sundials and primitive clocks to a reliable ship's chronometer, the mediaeval explorer could rove to the 'four corners of the earth'.

We can perceive in this a sort of evolving and reaching outwards that is very similar to that which we glimpsed through the medium of science-fiction imagery. As was observed, the direction of awareness is from the unconscious to the conscious state; from feeling and intuiting to thinking and knowing.

There is one thing that both the ancient systems of divination and world navigation have in common, and that is 'number'. The terrestrial and celestial co-ordinates use the numerical divisions of degrees, minutes, and seconds of arc, to measure space (not forgetting hours, minutes, and seconds of time measurement), while the ancients employed the mystical, qualitative, or 'inner power' of number to represent the deeper, philosophical concepts of life, as well as that which lies beyond life. Hence, we find, in early Chinese culture, numerical constructions of various geometric shapes, like 'magical' number squares, spirals and circles. The swastika shape, also used for number patterns, is interesting because, although in outline it is square, it is also suggestive of circular movement. Thus, a number series contained within this form takes on an even deeper and more profound symbolism. Squares formed from odd- and even-number series were constructed to represent the heavenly orders of the 'Earlier' and the 'Inner World', and the well-known divinatory system, the I Ching, is based entirely upon numbers; as too is the profound philosophy of life, Tao, or 'The Way'.

Numbers were used to represent the cardinal points, the seasons, the four elements, and so on. They were seen to relate to certain personality traits, and could be observed as indicating developments in time, thus serving as a medium for interpreting the 'will of heaven'. It is of interest to note, incidentally, that the words 'mathematician' and 'astrologer' were interchangeable about eight hundred years ago, as too were 'astronomer' and 'astrologer'. It is strange to reflect upon the fact that our whole advanced system of travel and space exploration is based upon a method of fortune-telling!

The instinctive urge to discover, to become, to reach Selfhood, is inseparable from the mundane need to achieve an orientation with the world we find ourselves in. Astrology, just because it has evolved out of such spiritual aspirations, and because it is numerically structured from the natural, rhythmic cycles of the universe, stands unique as a system for revealing Self at the Centre.

I used the word 'horoscope' in the heading of this chapter because it is probably better known than 'birth-chart' or 'cosmogram', although these latter words are in general use by practising astrologers and students. 'Horoscope' dates back to ancient Greece, when the present application and structure of today's birth-chart was beginning to evolve, though it was square rather than circular, as now. The literal meaning of horoscope is one who observes time (*hora* time + *skopos* observer). True, astrological procedure does involve the observation of a moment in time. A friend of mine in the Royal Air Force tells me that the recording of planetary positions relevant to a time and a place upon the earth's surface, i.e. the place of a birth, is rather like astro-navigation in reverse. By identifying particular planets in the night sky, and using astronomical reference tables, a pilot or navigator can fix his position. The astrologer already knows, of course, the co-ordinates (position) and time of a birth, and by referring to the tables can construct a map of the heavens, i.e. a birth-chart.

'Cosmogram' is a word that is being substituted more and more, because 'astrology' is a word that has become somewhat tainted by misuse, and is almost a source of embarrassment for many serious astrologers. Though, strictly speaking, the cosmogram, in its modern concept, is better known for its reference to the 'mid-point' system, a valuable development of traditional methods, based upon the observation of planetary complexes, than for the framework of the astrological houses, with the planets therein.

Everyday language actually contains many words that have an astrological origin. 'Consider' means with the stars, and 'influenza' means the influence of the stars. But, we may ask, do the stars actually influence us? We have reviewed some of the ways in which man's understanding has developed through the ages, and although, sadly, the mindlessness of mankind in the mass exhibits our lower nature in no uncertain terms, despite the euphemism of our so-called civilized society, the instinctive urge and direction is ever upwards into consciousness and light; the quest for knowledge continues to extend our mental and physical horizons.

A derivation of the word 'influence' may mean, as the dictionary tells us, a 'flowing from the stars', but even the early Greek philosophers were a little more discerning than that. They thought that we were able to see the stars because of something radiating from the eyes. In other words, their conception was that something travelled from us to the stars, and not the other way round. The explanation for such reasoning is easily understood when one realizes that it is in the nature of human beings to project part of their innermost feelings onto objects about them, and especially those feelings which cannot be readily accepted in themselves. I have dealt with this tendency in *Stress and the Sun Signs*, but an example may help you to understand more clearly what is meant by projection.

If you cannot tolerate weakness or timidity in others it is almost certain that there is a nucleus of fear in yourself, just below the surface of consciousness, lurking like an uneasy shadow. If you hate aggression excessively, while giving the impression of being a particularly placid individual, take heed of the Martian quality of your dreams, or the seemingly pointless, restless activity that fills your days. That which cannot be easily contained in ourselves is transferred to others. If you don't believe me, try listening, but in a quiet, unbiased, and detached manner, to a political discussion. Single out what it is that one side is so vehemently accusing the other side of doing or not doing. Quite a salutary lesson can be derived from this!

Today, we tend to scorn primitive peoples who believe that trees, rocks, lakes, and so on, contain spirits, dryads, and nymphs, and yet we still retain our 'gods' and 'demons', though they now go under different guises, and are expressed in terms like, 'anxiety state', 'insomnia', 'neuroticism'. These are just different modes of the same unconscious principle. The early philosophers knew instinctively that it wasn't Venus that directly stirred their feelings of love, or Mars their war-like tendencies, but they were not able to put into precise terms exactly what was the psychological process that gives rise to projection. Thanks to Jung we now have an adequate understanding of such behavioural tendencies, for which he also used the French term '*participation mystique*'. (*Man and His Symbols*.)

I have referred to the Sun's apparent path, or ecliptic, because it is the division of this circle that provides astrology with its physical and psychological framework, and reference for the orientation of life experience, just as in navigation the same divisions and coordinates provide grid references for one's orientation to the physical universe about us.

The Moon, too, establishes its impress upon the unconscious of mankind, becoming externalized in the mythology of the ages. Its twelve revolutions, giving the lunar month of 29½ days, almost coincide with the 365 days of the solar year. These cycles, along with the diurnal and nocturnal rhythm of light and dark alternating every twelve hours, are indelibly stamped upon the fabric of life. These are, of course, factual, astronomical references, constituting part of the science of astrology. How can we not be an integral part of the cosmos in which, for so brief a time we have our mundane existence? And if so, why should the horoscope or birth-chart not reflect the inner truth of our nature and being? Of course it does. We know this for a fact, even if we cannot yet explain all that is of the psyche in concrete, scientific terms.

However, the gaps in our understanding are bound to be filled before long, for even as I write this (in the spring of 1982), I have before me the second issue of a truly scientific publication on astrological research, entitled *Correlation*. For the first time ever, or so I believe, we have a journal dedicated entirely to presenting scientific papers of a high standard.

As soon as an acceptable method for gathering the statistical data required to demonstrate an unmistakable correlation between specific types of behaviour patterns, and their astrological correlates, has been established, we shall see a much wider acknowledgement of astrology's validity by the scientific body. A great deal of first-class research has already been carried out, notably by M. Gauquelin, Prof. H. Eysenck, Jeff Mayo, and others. The only real problem, to date, has been in formulating the actual methods for investigation that can be agreed upon.

There is a degree of irony in the present situation, because practising consultants, like myself, employ astrological techniques year in and year out, and know only too well that astrology 'works'. And yet it has taken the cynical attitude of the American group of scientists towards Gauquelin's painstaking researches, to stimulate other, more enlightened scientists, to actually start doing something tangible.

Nevertheless, even at this late stage, any positive approach by trained minds is to be applauded. There are some astrologers, of course, who take a rather guarded view of scientists intruding upon their subject. These, usually, tend to be of an esoteric inclination, and generally of the opinion that 'higher knowledge' should not be debased by mundane considerations.

The majority of astrologers, however, firmly believe that the pursuit of truth and knowledge is of prior importance, as too is the demonstration of the practical application of astrology in society. The increase in the number of summer courses at universities on astrological subjects and counselling bears witness to this, as too does the spread of astrological instruction at Centres of Further Education; an area which I pioneered and am now pleased to see is growing steadily.

If there is difficulty in setting up adequate parameters for researching the birth-chart, can you imagine the problem scientists will have in presenting feasible proof of astrological prognostication! For convenience of explanation, forecasting in astrology can be broadly divided into two categories, 'causal', and 'acausal', to borrow from the terminology of science. The first lends itself comparatively easily to scientific investigation, assuming, of course, the initial acceptance of the astrological concept of there being some sort of planetary 'influence'. By observing the actual, forward movement of the heavenly bodies, by reference to their positions as given in the astronomical tables, for any time in the future, and relating these to the original blue-print, i.e. birth-chart, it is then possible to make relevant deductions from the new or forming angular relationships.

I should, perhaps, explain briefly that particular angles between planets, and planets and earth, are what most demonstrably affect human responses. The same angular relationships produce radio 'interference' and 'static'. These movements are termed 'transits' by astrologers, and from them the type of responses, as well as the areas of life experience involved, can be inferred. As the current or actual movement of any body is being observed, we can reason that if there is a corresponding response in the individual, in accord with traditional interpretation, then the response may be said to have had a cause. It then remains for the investigator to prove that this response was not produced, say, by a change in temperature, or by any other environmental condition. No easy task, by any means, but it does lend itself to the fundamental, scientific principle of causality.

The second category of astrological forecasting is much more difficult to establish on purely scientific grounds because it operates in that nebulous area of the archetypes of the collective unconscious (Jung: *Collected Works*, vol. 9.i.) previously referred to as irrepresentable, 'morphic resonance', and so on. We may term this category 'acausal', though giving it a decent, scientific title doesn't make the task of extracting provable facts any easier. Besides looking at 'transits' to a chart, astrologers also observe 'progressions' of the chart. I will be telling you a little more about these in the next chapter. Here, suffice it to say that they are symbolic counts or measures of planetary movements, having no reference to the actual, physical movement, in time and space.

The process of interpretation is similar to that employed by 'readers' of the Tarot, I Ching, runes, and so on. However, there is a significant difference that sets astrology apart. Most forms of divination involve the apparently random, physical action of casting or selecting objects. The only random thing in astrology is birth, and the fact that we have no choice in the matter of exactly when we are to be born. Yet, the time of birth is a factual reference point, an interception of a life-force into the constant, cyclic fluxion of the Universe.

Computer-calculated, astronomical tables provide the astrologer with an accurate reference to the movements of Sun, Moon, and planets, for as far back or forward in time as one wishes to go. There is, therefore, a well established set of guidelines which can be followed with comparative ease, and these can be applied, symbolically, to the life pattern. I think the simplest way to describe this to you is to present an analogy or two. The birth-chart itself has often been likened to a blue-print. The skilled craftsman or technician is able to visualize from such a drawing exactly what the finished product will look like, and how it will function. To you and me it would appear to be a jumble of lines and figures. By projecting (progressing) the birth-chart positions of the planets forwards, symbolically, but with the aid of the astronomical tables, it is possible to visualize the likely experiences of the individual personality.

This is just the same as holding an acorn in your hand, and imagining it as a full-grown tree. You will have a general idea of what it will look like because you are familiar with the shape of oak trees. You will know, too, that in the winter it will lose its leaves, and be reasonably certain that new buds will burst forth the following spring. You may even have a vague idea of the length of life of an oak, but not much else. However, if you happened to be an arboriculturist, knowledgeable in the cultivation of trees, you would be aware of its species, which location it thrived in best, how the environment might impede or encourage its growth, the ultimate shape of the branches as they reach out into the surrounding space, and so on. In short, you will have reliable foreknowledge of a great many facts about the *expectant* life pattern of that acorn. Because of specialist training, the astrologer is capable of making similar deductions from known facts. Those facts — the symbolism of established, astronomical patterns — can be traced like ornamental paving-stones along a winding garden-path.

You will notice that I say 'expectant life pattern'. This is to underline the point made previously, that no astrologer, as such, expects to do more than assess tendencies and conjecture probable outcomes. In other words, to forecast trends, and not to predict events. Naturally, there are those whose approach is biased towards intuition rather than intellect.

I remember hearing Maurice Woodruff, a world-famous clairvoyant, explaining that he sometimes used the horoscope, but rather in the same way as he would consult tea leaves, crystal ball or cards. They were simply a medium for concentrating his attention, and for assisting in achieving a rapport with the person consulting him.

I find, in my classes, that students fall roughly into two groups. Some will cope well with the calculations and extensive detail of chart analysis, and be able to draw meaningful conclusions from what they see in the chart. If they have kept their reasoning close to the interpretation of each symbol, as taught, their deductions will be accurate because it is in the nature of astrology to reveal graphically the actuality of response and experience as potentialities for being and becoming. And then there are those who just cannot seem to handle the mathematics, and the need to construct neat, clear charts for orderly interpretation is just anathema to them! But, it is often these people who are the most intuitive, and who have a natural ability to 'tune-in' to the very area we find so hard to define. Parapsychologists have been working in this field of the paranormal quite extensively, but it is still a comparatively young science, having to struggle with the daunting task of endeavouring to make sense of the will-o'-the-wisp qualities of acausal principles.

I have touched broadly upon the use of symbols, and the fact that the important ones are impressed, as it were, upon the collective unconscious of mankind. As 'archetypal images' they may be perceived as the material of dreams, or as projections of civilization's strong, emotional contents, which takes form in the mythology of the world. Initially, a symbol comes into being when there is something to be expressed, but which cannot be directly put into thought or word. Thus, an image, geometric form, or figure, is generated from psychic (emotional) energy, which has an analogous quality.

In selecting an example, Saturn is a clear choice as it has long been associated with our concept of 'Time', particularly in the guise of 'Father Time', holding a sickle. This figure embodies much of our innermost feelings about the abstract qualities of time and its inexorable passing; the long struggle for existence (especially for early man), the cold of winter and the shortage of food, when time must have hung like an eternity, and life itself stood in the balance until the fresh crops became available.

The ceaseless toil that marked the hours of daylight, gave a means to sustain life, but also a reason for living during the so-brief period we are upon the earth, and which must inevitably reach the end of its cycle. Hence, the same figure is also called the 'Grim Reaper', symbolizing the visitation of death. In ancient times, of course, the successful balance of life and death was directly influenced by the growth or failure of crops, and the effectiveness of the work-effort. Saturn was depicted by the Romans as a god of agriculture, carrying a bill-hook, and later, in Greek mythology, appeared as Cronos, the father of Zeus.

Because the period of the year most in accord with all our primordial impressions of time weighing heavily was at the winter equinox (21st December), when daylight is shortest and the Sun moves into the sign of Capricorn, Saturn became associated with this sign, and so it is that astrologers talk of Saturn being the 'ruler' of Capricorn. At this time of the year, too, the Romans held their festival of Saturnalia. In the Northern hemisphere, great fires were lit, marking similar festive occasions, and, no doubt, relieving the gloom and cold, besides serving as a welcome reminder of the spring to come as the days lengthened.

This is the way in which symbols evolve. No matter in what age or part of the world, human beings all share the same, basic feelings. Our deepest, strongest emotions always find expression in symbols. The essential meaning of a symbol will therefore always be the same, even if the form varies from one culture to another, and one individual to another. Sometimes, one hears astrologers referring to Saturn as 'he', or to some other planet as 'she'. Attributing human characteristics to heavenly bodies is natural, certainly, but such references have to be observed with great care, especially by those who are expected to make objective deductions. Chart analysis, just like psycho-analysis, requires that the analyst, though having compassion and understanding, does not interject a subjective view, and thus distort the truth of the chart pattern.

By the same token, no one chart feature should be singled out at the expense of the remainder. If the astrologer who interpreted the horoscope of the lady I mentioned earlier had not thrust the dismal side of Saturn to the fore, astrology alone need not have been blamed for causing her 'break-down'. Saturn is, perhaps, the most often misrepresented and misunderstood of all the planets that students of astrology have to familiarize themselves with.

Just because the dictionaries, when quoting the astrological view, tend to emphasize the gloom and doom aspect of Saturn's symbolism, it is no excuse for avoiding a balanced consideration of all its qualities. Or rather, all those below-consciousness impresses which, in composite, externalize in the mythological symbolism of Saturn. For example, time also brings maturity and experience, and so another facet of Saturn, projected in human form, is that of the 'Wise Old Man'. In this guise it can be found in mythology, and was recognized by Jung, who came across it often enough in the dream analyses of his patients.

In the astrological model, Saturn has come to represent the natural limits of self-awareness in the individual personality. Here, it is suggestive of instinctive caution, without which there would be an absence of a proper sense of discretion and constraint. Jeff Mayo's definition (*The Planets and Human Behaviour*) offers a sensible assessment: its function is ''To develop *self-control* through formative processes requiring a sense of method and purpose, self-reliance and discipline, realistic and constructive thinking.''

Saturn, as a point at which the crystallization of ego-consciousness takes place, is an important factor in the planetary hierarchy of the horoscope. The chart (horoscope) as a whole is representative of personality as a whole, existing in time and space; the Saturnian function is, therefore, seen as the precipitation of the awareness of self, and the consolidation of identity in relationship with the environment. In actuality, we attain our sense of self through our life's work, or vocation. Saturn, as we have seen, is related to this area, too, but vocation, as a life-orienting function, is also a Capricornian principle, and I shall be explaining something of this to you when we review the symbolism of the Zodiac in Chapter 5.

4. FORECASTING IN ASTROLOGY

Early one morning I was woken by the sound of the telephone. It was a call from Fiji! A client for whom I had solved a business problem felt she just had to ring to tell me that her sailing date was exactly when I had said it would be. I had mentioned this quite casually when replying to a letter from her in which she told me the date booked for her passage from Fiji to Australia. Glancing quickly at her chart I had noticed a significant aspect, involving Neptune (the sea), which occured a week or so after the date she had given. This proved to be the very day she sailed. Apparently, when she bought her ticket at the shipping office they had actually given her the wrong date.

This episode occurred soon after I turned professional, and as a forecast it was just as impressive for me as for the good lady who had phoned all that distance. In the normal course of events I would not have attempted to make a specific prediction because consultation is about rather more profound considerations than that, but it does illustrate how surprisingly accurate astrological observation can be. However, let me make it quite clear that few planetary aspects form so precisely on time, or correlate so neatly with the event. More often, it is a question of assessing a whole series of aspects, and endeavouring to conjecture likely *tendencies* in the life pattern as a whole.

Until comparatively recent times the general impression was that astrology was simply a method for prediction or forecasting, and little else. I suppose part of the blame for this erroneous view must be placed upon the shoulders of those medieval astronomers who augmented their incomes by practising the art of fortune-telling. That they should have had knowledge of astrology is no great surprise for the two subjects were at one time inseparable. Until about the time of the Middle Ages most of the world's great

Universities taught astronomy and astrology together. The latter fell into disrepute, no doubt because of the inept way it was employed; students of astronomy are not necessarily the most efficient astrological consultants. Debased as a fortune-telling medium, astrology became further diffused and distorted as it fell from the hands of scientists into those of the fair-ground soothsayers.

Not until the emergence of psychology as an accepted science for the study of human behaviour, was the significance of astrology as a highly sophisticated method of analysis and typology fully realized. As we have seen, the birth-chart can be thought of as a blue print of life in potential. Therefore, as a forecasting system in its most elementary form, and without any further additions or calculations to the natal chart, basic inferences can be made as to the probable development of the personality. And because the chart is so constructed as to reflect an individual's likely orientation, a conjecture of the potential for specific areas of life experience is also possible. There are many students who, not wishing or able to pursue the complexities of 'progressed' charts, are quite satisfied in evaluating life potentials without having to cope with lengthy calculations for indicating periods of probable manifestation.

The most commonly used method for adjusting birth-charts in time, past, present or future, is that known as 'Secondary Directions'. This employs the 'day for a year' principle, and it is fairly straightforward to put up a 'progressed' chart by referring to the standard ephemeris or astronomical calendar for the year of birth, and counting on, from the birth date, the number of days equivalent to the number of years in the life. The new planetary positions are then related to their original places, and deductions made. It is generally thought that these, progressed to birth or natal positions, reflect alterations in the developing temperament.

An example of this method is to be found in the chart of that fine British actress, Glenda Jackson. At the time she announced the separation from her husband, in May 1975, Venus (feelings of relatedness and affection) had progressed to a position where it made an angular contact or aspect with Saturn (feelings of restriction and standing alone). As you can see, astrological interpretation can be fairly explicit, even when keeping to the literal meanings of symbols. Yet caution must always be observed, for symbolism abounds with ambiguities. For example, the same combination of planets could equally well produce a strong sense of loyalty, because alternative connotations in Saturn's meaning are constraint and responsibility. Every positive has its negative value, and symbolism does no more than reveal the law of opposites that is inherent throughout nature.

Once the progressions have been attended to, the next step is to observe the 'Transits'. Planetary positions, past, current, or future, can be referred to, using the astronomical calendar for the period under consideration. No extra calculations are necessary, and it is a simple matter to observe any angular contacts made by a transiting planet to one in the birth-chart. It is thought that transits appear to correlate with the flux of events, and the press of circumstances upon the conglomerate of emotions that are to be found in any individual.

A quite recent example of a transit in operation is before me as I write (4th May 1982). Tracing the current path of Saturn, I found that it reached the degree in the ecliptic where the natal Sun of Mrs Margaret Thatcher, British Prime Minister, was placed at the time of her birth, exactly on 1st April 1982. In astrological terminology, "transiting Saturn came to a conjunction with the natal Sun." The date, you may recall, was when the trouble in the Falkland Islands was announced.

If we take an interpretation of this combination from the textbook (*Teach Yourself Astrology*) of an accepted authority, Jeff Mayo, we find, "Conjunction: develops powerful self-disciplinary patterns of behaviour . . . responsible, practical, resourceful . . ." Another, equally notable authority is Reinhold Ebertin, and we find in his little book *Transits*, ". . . estrangement, separations . . . professional difficulties."

The natal disposition of Saturn in Mrs Thatcher's chart is, fortunately, of a positive nature, implying immense determination and resolve in the pursuit of objectives. If we apply this to the Falkland crisis it could be an encouraging indication. Naturally, a mundane or political astrologer would require a great deal more material to work on than this, and would be perusing the inceptional charts of the countries concerned, as well as those of all the leading personalities involved.

In standard practice, therefore, an astrological forecast requires, as a minimum, the study of natal, progressed, and transiting aspects. This usually entails a considerable amount of work, and, obviously, fees are charged by qualified professionals to cover the time involved. I am informed, however, that some commercial astrologers never trouble with progressions because of the length of time required for their calculation and interpretation. If this is so, then, to my mind, it is gross malpractice, but until governments establish registers of qualified practitioners, and enforce a clearly defined code of practice, astrology will continue to suffer in the hands of non-professionals.

Although progressions and transits might be considered as minimum requirements upon which to base conjecture as to future tendencies, there are several other factors which, although constituents of a developing chart pattern, can be viewed separately, as useful indicators and measures of life trends. For example, the periodic cycle of Moon and Saturn can be observed in terms of a person's urge to establish a sense of self-identity; to be a particular being. Or, Venus and Mars, as the cycle of the reproductive urge.

Of all the various cycles of planetary pairs, that of the Sun and Moon is the most important. The soli-lunar cycle, in a curious way, appears to mark transitionary stages in life. Because, in astrology, we have the precept that 'A day equals a year', the lunar month, of approximately twenty-nine days, can be visualized as twenty-nine years. The symbolism is based upon the phases of the Moon, from New to Full, and back to New again, when one cycle ends and another begins.

The first 'Great Cycle' can be considered as relating to the development of personal abilities. The second will usually see the establishment of the self in society, and the third 'Great Cycle', commencing from approximately age 58, is, ideally, the phase in which the inner and spiritual life begins to take on a greater significance.

It is interesting to observe how these symbolic, soli-lunar phases so closely parallel the recognized periods in life when increased psychological tensions can be expected. For instance, if the young adult has not found a suitable vocation, or has not, in one way or another, matured satisfactorily by around the thirtieth year, emotional disturbances can sometimes arise at this time or during the following few years. That is to say, around the time of the first progressed New Moon, to some four years later when the Moon enters its Crescent phase, which is again coincident with a particular angle of relationship between Sun and Moon. (This angle is known to astronomers and astrologers as a semi-square, or 45 degree angle.)

The second period in life that often sees some difficulties occurs around the forty-fifth year. This actually coincides with the Full Moon phase, when, as you will know, Sun and Moon appear opposite each other, and the Moon reflects the full light of the Sun upon the night-dark earth. Here is a time of reaching fulfilment, of seeing more clearly what lies ahead, as seen in the light of past experience. But if reasonable satisfaction with life is not present at this time, then it is easier to suffer a period of inner tension or dissatisfaction with self or life, or both.

In the literal sense, there is a two-way pull, symbolized, of course, in the opposition of Sun and Moon. And as these bodies also relate to the archetypal male and female images, the mid-life period can also be a sensitive one where relationships are concerned. Incidentally, although the 'change of life' usually occurs around the same time, it is more often related, astrologically, to transiting Uranus (symbolic of change and disruption) coming to the opposition of its own natal place in the birth-chart.

The value of cycles in forecasting is that they enable the astrologer to assess the main trends of the life pattern, common to us all, thus providing a broader perspective to the birth-chart and personality as a whole. The fact that difficult or critical episodes can occur at specific periods in a lifetime is, of course, generally accepted, and well known to psychologists and others. We might say that what is 'prognostication' for the astrologer is 'prognosis' for the therapist!

With Horary astrology we come to a system much more akin to fortune-telling. It was greatly favoured and widely practised during the Middle Ages, and is still popular today as an alternative form of divination. It differs from its modern counterpart in that chart calculation is based, not upon the time of birth or inception, but when a question begins to beat upon the consciousness of the enquirer, demanding an answer.

There are those who believe that the time to be used for Horary charts is when the enquirer actually puts the question to the astrologer. In one book of instruction, for example, the suggestion is given that "we take the exact time when the question was verbally expressed, the opening of a mailed enquiry, or the time the problem came by phone." The writer had obviously drawn upon the somewhat confused discourses that have passed down the centuries.

Horary, with its fixed rules of interpretation, can be likened to the I Ching, Tarot, or any other form of divination that requires a clearly defined procedure within which an apparently random distribution takes place. And, as I have explained previously, such methods can be viewed quite simply as instruments for revealing contents of the unconscious, both personal and collective.

In this respect, Margaret Hone's (*The Modern Textbook of Astrology*) observation is relevant and explanatory: "In moments of stress and anxiety, a person seems to feel that he has correlation with something outside himself. It may be that this instinctive feeling springs from his unconscious knowledge of his oneness with the universe, and as the saying goes, 'the question asks him' rather than that he asks the question."

We might say, therefore, that Horary is a communing with the cosmos in order to find the answer to some urgent problem. Hence, the crucial factor here is not when the astrologer is posed the question, but, surely, the actual time the individual was spurred into seeking a solution.

Most people are familiar with the twelve Sun-signs, and know that their birth date falls when the sun is in a particular part of the ecliptic circle, i.e. the apparent path of the sun, throughout the year. In this, the circle of 360 degrees becomes divided into sectors of 30 degrees each, so that, when we talk of the sun being, for example, in Aries, we really mean that it is moving through the first 30 degrees of the circle. At the 30 degree point it moves into Taurus, at the 60 degree point, into Gemini, and so on. Thus, interpretation of the signs of the Zodiac is actually a reference to degree areas within the circle.

Hence, in astrology, we are really dealing with numerical values, as much as anything. It has been found that each sector can be subdivided into three, each giving an additional shade of meaning to the sign, and greater accuracy to the interpretation of the signs, as has been clearly demonstrated in my book *Stress and the Sun-Signs*.

Further sub-divisions of the circle can be made, and each can be seen to reflect a certain attribute or facet, to the overall interpretation. In the 'Sabian Symbols' we have an interpretation of each of the 360 degrees. The symbolism for these was originally derived from the intuitive interpretation of Marc Edmund Jones, and a clairvoyant friend, many years ago. By combining the astrological symbolism of the degrees with ordinary playing-cards, Dane Rudhyar evolved a simple but effective divinatory system which he called 'An Astrological Mandala'. (See *Bibliography*.) Here, therefore, is a simplified form of astrological divination that is on a par with the I Ching, or any other form of fortune-telling that relies upon some physical activity.

That, of course, is not true astrology, and is hardly comprehensive in the amount of detailed information it is able to reveal. Moving still further into a simplification of applied astrology we come to the Solarscope, commonly used by the purveyors of popular astrology to magazines and periodicals. Many serious astrologers object strongly to this form of astrological forecasting, but I believe that the majority of readers know well enough that 'Your Stars For The Day' is nothing more than an entertainment feature. I suspect, too, that newspaper editors consider star columns as being merely useful space fillers!

Interestingly enough, it is easy for anyone with some knowledge of astrology, and a handy astronomical calendar, to see whether or not these 'Star Forecasts' have been compiled by a competent astrologer, or the office junior! Judging by some of the daily predictions, the story that they are written by a reporter with nothing better to do, holds some credence.

It is the women's magazines that usually feature the best of the starscopes for the masses, although these can vary considerably. My wife, for instance, considers one long established astrological contributor to be ''very good'', while dismissing the rest with a terse ''rubbish!'' The Solarscope is based upon the monthly Sun-signs, each of which are placed, in turn, against the Eastern horizon line at the '1st House' position of a pre-set horoscope wheel, with its twelve 'House' divisions of life experiences or orientation.

Because the placing of each sign against a provisional 1st House simulates a birth that would normally be about 5 a.m. to 6 a.m., there is just a chance that someone who is born around dawn may find that the forecast will have some relevance, perhaps in indicating an area of life which is, in fact, being stirred up in some way. Even so, I am sure it will be obvious to you that Solarscopes, by their very nature, are too generalized to take seriously. Not that the majority of people do take the 'Fun With The Stars' columns and features seriously, anyway.

A word of warning, however, about an area of commercialized astrology that can be taken seriously by the uninformed. Some magazines carry advertisements for computerized horoscopes, and it is as well if you know what is meant by this. If it means that the horoscope (birth-chart) has been calculated with the aid of a computer, there is certainly nothing wrong with this, other than the fact that computers can and do make errors due to faulty pro-gramming. If, on the other hand, the advertisement conveys to you the idea that, for just a few pounds or dollars, you will receive a computerized 'reading' of your horoscope, or a ''forecast for the year ahead'', then you have every right to be suspicious.

It is perfectly possible to programme a computer with set interpretations of the planets in each of the signs and Houses, and the aspects between each and every planet, as well as the hundred-and-one other factors that an astrologer has to take into consideration. But the computer cannot assess the subtle modifications that the total imposes upon each separate item, cannot view the personality as modified by its environment, and certainly is unable to discuss, clarify or enlarge upon a pressing human problem. The cost of such a reading may well seem cheap compared with the services of a professional astrologer, but is in reality exceedingly dear when you discover the true value of what you have received for your money, in terms of guidance, advice, insight into personal problems, and so on.

This chapter would not be complete without a brief reference to 'The Age of Aquarius'. Most people have heard the phrase, and may have a vague idea that it has something to do with our entry into this modern era, though they may know little else about this rather intriguing and mysterious appellation. It refers, in fact, to part of a vast time cycle that has its origins in an astronomical phenomenon, and its symbolism in astrological connotation. The spin of the earth produces the familiar day and night rhythm, but the earth also teeters on its axis, rather like a top when it slows down. This results in the North Pole describing a circle in the heavens, just as the apex of a top performs its gyrations in the air.

It takes the Pole approximately 25,000 years to complete one circle, and this has been termed a 'Great Year'. It is divided into twelve periods of about 2,000 years each, and these appear to accord remarkably well with the attributes of the signs. Because the movement of the Pole is backward in relation to the constellations, the corresponding references to the signs are also in reverse order.

It is easy enough to observe relevant tendencies in each of the 2,000-year sign periods, and assess their correlation with world history. For example, about 2000 B.C. it could be concluded that we were moving from a Taurean to an Arien Age. The Mithraic, Sacred Bull of the previous age was now being superseded by the Ram, whose horns were commonly displayed on soldiers' helmets. This was a time that witnessed a surge of pioneering spirit, and resounded to the clash of arms and the thud of Arien battering-rams. The Golden Calf fell into disfavour, and the sacrificial lamb took its place.

It has been observed that Christianity marked the dawn of the Piscean Age, and certainly it is a curious coincidence that fish, compassion, sorrow, and sacrifice are synonymous with both.

Equally, we can reason that the Industrial Revolution, the rapid progress into high technology, and the extraordinary leap forward of scientific knowledge in a comparatively short space of time, must herald the Age of Aquarius. Those of us who have long been aware of this broad symbolism of the Great Year, have watched enthralled as each step forward of mankind's technical ability reveals itself to the wondering world, like an audience waiting with bated breath as one spectacular event follows another, against the backdrop of space and time in an ever-evolving universe.

Thus, the application of astrology as a forecasting system varies considerably, from detailed analyses that are on a par with meteorological weather projections, to the augural strictures of gloom-mongers who, at the drop of a planet, will predict fire, flood, or general devastation. As in all crafts, it is not the tool that should be in question, but the manner in which it is employed.

5. THE INTEGRATED LIFE CYCLE

Throughout the world's long history the 'Human Condition' has ever been a major consideration for wise men, oracles, and philosophers. Religious and sociological experience is founded upon such fundamental questions as: "What is the meaning of life?" or "Who am I?" Astrology, no less, is a product of human consciousness, born out of the need to understand in order to survive.

The eternal, cyclic rhythm of the universe leaves its inevitable impress upon the consciousness of man, whether we are aware of it or not. The developing symbolism of the Zodiac keeps pace with the evolution of civilizations, ever adapting, ever appropriate to the era or country, simply because the consciousness of mankind is itself forever evolving out of the collective unconscious from which it originally sprang. This continual adaptation of all symbols can be more clearly understood if we recall that not a century ago 'visions' still consisted of religious images, as, for example, the 'Angels of Mons' of the 1914-1918 war.

Gradually, as technology provided society with greater independence and freedom from nature's harsh demands, man felt himself to be master of his universe, and God slipped into the background. In no time at all, modern man, just like his early predecessors, conjured up suitable images to fill the void, and projected them into the heavens. But now they were rather more sophisticated. No longer was it sufficient that planets should be gods and goddesses, or even imposing angels descending upon fluffy white clouds. Now it had to be visitors from outer space, flying saucers, or unidentified flying objects. The nomenclature 'UFO' has about it a vagueness that is associated with dream material and synonymous with the ambiguity of the archetypal images of the unconscious.

It could be argued, of course, that all symbols have an ambiguity, or rather, an ambivalence, since they are conscious manifestations

THE INTEGRATED LIFE CYCLE

of those powerful feelings that cannot easily be expressed in other forms. All emotions contain within them the potential for their opposite quality. Laughter is often close to tears, love and hate can go hand in hand, and over-activity may well bring about a complete reversal in the form of inertia or depression. Thus, the signs of the Zodiac, for all their archaic nature, may be seen to contain a symbolism that is entirely relevant to the needs and inherent self-expression of mankind today, with its 'status symbols' in the shape of the latest fashion or technological 'gimmick'.

The first sign to start the cycle of life (*see diagram on p. 58*), is Aries, containing the essence of spiritual fire, and the initiatory quality that benefits the springing into existence of new endeavour. The Sun enters Aries at the vernal equinox, 21st March, from which time the days begin to lengthen, and new life stirs within the soil.

This flickering flame has yet to find substance and stability in Taurean earth, and seeks to find its identity by imposing itself, hither-and-thither, upon the objects about it. The interplay of 'I' and 'Thou' that can be perceived in the Arien personality, with its sometimes tempestuous responses in relationships, is reflected clearly in the symbolism of the Aries — Libra polarization. Because it has yet to establish a sense of self, the Arien temperament covers its insecurity in a flurry of assertive activity; with energy to combat uncertainty or anxiety.

By early spring the new shoots are breaking through the warming earth, the sun rises higher each day, and there is a feeling of oneness with nature. Energy now begins to take on form, and power infuses bio-structures with the urge to proliferate, not now with fiery, Arien impetuosity, but with organic purpose. The 'down-to-earth' Taurean proceeds with quiet determination to fecundate both environment and species. Here is the instinctive, biological urge of the feeling nature that in its Scorpionic polarization will find expression in the emotive drive that spurs the individual to become intimately involved in the strivings of society.

Late spring sees further growth, and now the young plants are complete organisms, reaching out into the air and responding to the light. This is the Geminian, school-child period of learning, finding out, and inquisitively investigating all that is going on. The mind is acquiring knowledge but has yet to reach the intellectual maturity and vision that is to be found in its Sagittarian complement.

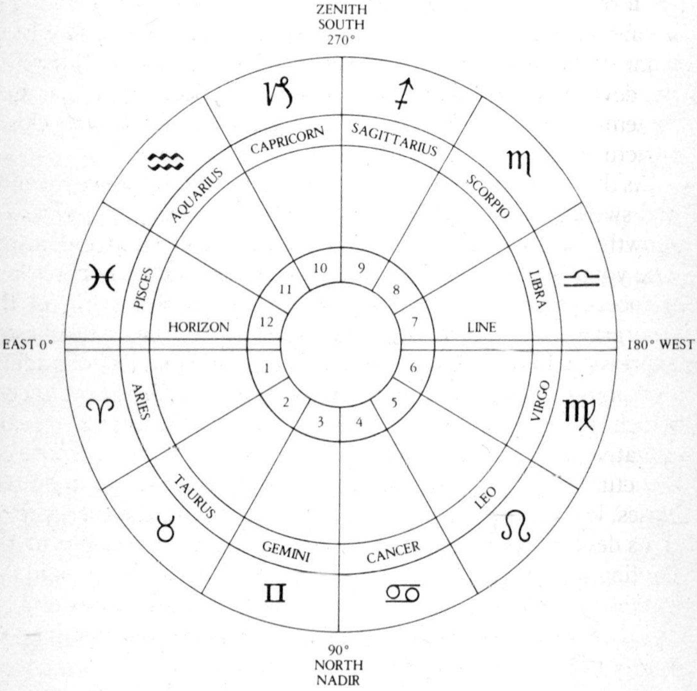
ZENITH
SOUTH
270°
EAST 0°
180° WEST
90°
NORTH
NADIR
HORIZON
LINE
CAPRICORN
SAGITTARIUS
SCORPIO
LIBRA
VIRGO
LEO
CANCER
GEMINI
TAURUS
ARIES
PISCES
AQUARIUS
1
2
3
4
5
6
7
8
9
10
11
12

THE INTEGRATED LIFE CYCLE

With the advent of the summer solstice, the young buds of spring become fertile flowers, and there is a focalization of the life-force. Typifying this is Cancerian concentration, and desire for well-defined boundaries of experience. In the growing child these have yet to be structured and stabilized in the process of Capricornian crystallization. The Cancerian love of private, home life has to be sustained by the public life of career and vocation. As you can see from the diagram, Cancer is at the base of a cross, the arms of which are formed by Aries and Libra. Having the principle of 'four', in numerological terms, this configuration of equinoctial and solstice points imbues the life with an archetypal framework around which the developing personality will become moulded. Four, you may remember, relates to a ''model of wholeness in all relatively closed structures of human consciousness and in the body.''

As the sun moves into Leo, and with each fruit of nature ripening and swelling in the golden glow of high summer, the process of growth takes on a more meaningful and individualized colouring. The youngster, still basking and blossoming in the mother's love (Cancer), now feels, through the persistent prompting of the emerging ego and forming persona, the strong desire to satisfy self-expression. Play-time becomes recreation, and that tenuous admix of feelings, thoughts, and emotions (Taurus, Gemini, Cancer), which go to make up the ego-consciousness, begins to take tentative shape. The miracle of a new, organized personality structure reveals itself, as demanding of attention as our impulsive Aries, but now with an ego-centring that directs the energy flow. This developing desire for self-expression, ensnared as it is by the confines of family life, has yet to find satisfying fulfilment, and this it will eventually achieve in the wider environs of society, as signified by the complementary Aquarian phase of dissemination, where individuality may be fully realized.

With the Virgoan harvest-time comes adolescence, and the impress of the outer world begins to reach over the horizon. (*See diagram*.) What has been acquired, learnt, and experienced so far, is now collated into personal potentiality, to be rationalized and directed into some practical form. The function of every individual is to give something to society, and this is most commonly achieved by the work we do as our contribution to the welfare and benefit of others.

Should the ego-centring of Leo encroach too much upon Virgoan service, then the natural progression towards selfless giving through work — note the polarizing effect of Piscean self-sacrifice here — becomes stifled. Work is then seen only as that which satisfies material needs. Endless problems, affecting both the health and the work life, can arise from a maladjustment of attitude in this phase. This is true, not only of individuals, but also, in the collective sense, of the health of a country or nation.

Typical of the Virgoan principle is the desire for well ordered conditions, with efficiently working organisms and organizations. The true harvest of Virgo is the coming to fruition of selfhood, with all its unique talents, training, and technical skills, formulated if not yet tried and tested in the world at large. Both in a literal and a symbolic sense this phase may be seen to hold the potential for crisis or change, as the young person reaches the cross-roads to adulthood, and the sun moves irrevocably towards the horizon of autumn.

With the coming of the autumnal equinox the solar-force moves over the Western arm of the Zodiacal cross, into the upper quadrant of the circle. Youth has now more directly to react and respond to the outer world, and much will depend upon how effectively and harmoniously interrelationships can be made. The equalization of light and dark at the fall of the year, symbolized in the Libran scales, reflects clearly the constant necessity for balance in society if life for everyone is to be reasonably happy and smooth running. And yet, the Arien "Me first!" has somehow to be reconciled with Libran awareness of the fact that others matter, too. This transverse coupling of the East-West angles of the Zodiac plays a fundamental part in the motivation of the organism towards social orientation.

As personality develops and perceives greater dimensions of itself through the inter-action with others, it becomes necessary to somehow preserve its integrity in order not to "dissolve into the unconscious of the community." (Jung — *Modern Man In Search of a Soul*.) Emotions (Scorpio), as well as material and organic structures (Taurus), have also to be preserved, and so we find there is a natural instinct in mankind to keep secrets. Secret rites and ceremonies have been kept throughout history. And so we find that the tendencies of the Scorpionic phase are secretiveness, and a striving to contain or control. Characteristic of the urge to gain emotional control is the domination of the matador over the bull. Similar externalizations of the profound, archetypal urge to contain and control the more violent forces of nature, are to be found throughout the behaviour patterns of society.

In the Scorpionic phase, emotional criteria tend to overshadow other considerations, but human beings have a mental as well as a bio-physical response to their surroundings, and with the next sign, Sagittarius, the intellectual potential has an opportunity to reach full expression. The basic facts and details of knowledge, so assiduously absorbed in the Geminian phase, now attain transcedence in the imaginative intellect and philosophical insight of the well rounded personality. Thinking and imagining, while being attributes in themselves, can, if there is too much vacillation between the two, bring about an over-extension or exaggeration of ideas and views. Yet planning and idealism give depth and meaning to our lives, and without Sagittarian vision we are ill-prepared for future growth and expansion.

By the 21st December the shortest day is reached, and the sun enters Capricorn, once again to return from its southern declination with the promise of the new life to come. With the transit of the sun from Sagittarius into Capricorn, the zenith of the Zodiacal wheel is illumined, and it is as if the apex of the cosmic cross becomes vivified, bringing a conscious actualization to the configuration of signs. All that had been planned and prepared for in the Sagittarian phase is now given material form. With the coming of this winter solstice it is as if Christ is re-born each year. The festivities and ceremonies of Christmas-time bear witness to mankind's instinctive response to this deep, universal urge; life must be given a meaning and a purpose.

This purpose is reflected in the qualities of industriousness and ambition associated with the Capricornian personality. For every individual, purpose is embodied in the inner voice of the soul, and it is this 'voca' which whispers their vocation to those who listen.

A brief reference to the Taurus, Virgo, Capricorn triad may be of interest to you, since anything to do with the 'work ethic' is apposite with regard to the present world recession. The three signs form a triangle, and 'three', you will recall, has the quality of "progressive actualization in human consciousness." Thus, for the proper maintenance of the organic whole, it is essential to preserve the dynamic balance between the material manipulation of Taurus, and the efficient, Virgoan utilization of resources, in order that a firm and secure structure, with Capricornian aspiration at its pinnacle, may evolve.

It could be reasoned that a reversal from positive to negative expression of any of these three sign values would have a deleterious effect, whether the sense of purpose is seen as a personal one, or that of society as a whole. For example, an over accentuation of the Taurean need for material security and stability could result in avarice and inertia. A poorly integrated Virgoan concept of selfless service might lead to selfish inefficiency. Clearly, any distortion of such foundations would eventually topple the pinnacle. With no Capricornian sense of objectivity the individual, or society, lacks direction and balance; confusion and chaos must surely follow. In an age when it seems to be the mass rather than the individual that is catered for, the concept of work as a 'calling' has become obscured, and this is a sad thing, for — as Jung observed — ''Vocation is the thing that distinguishes the individual from the mass.''

Capricorn, because it is the 10th sign (the qualitative value of which number signifies the beginning of a new cycle of endeavour), and is placed at the peak of the triangle and cross formations, besides marking the high point or zenith of the sun's southern declination, is, indeed, a matrix of mankind's striving for Self-Realization.

The fact that the sun's zenith is in the Southern hemisphere, resulting in the dark of Northern winter, may appear to be a little paradoxical in terms of human experience, but its symbolism is explicit enough, for it is only by the most resolute attempts to search in the dim, dark recesses of the private self that the light is discovered, and the message of the inner voice becomes illumined with understanding. In this wise, one cannot do better than to reflect upon the words from Book 3 of the Hindu Vedantic classic *Bhagavad Gita*:

> He who sits suppressing all the instruments of flesh,
> Yet in his idle heart thinking on them,
> Plays the inept and guilty hypocrite:
> But he who, with strong body serving mind,
> Gives up his mortal powers to worthy work,
> Not seeking again, Arjuna! such an one
> Is honourable. Do thine allotted task!
> Work is more excellent than idleness;
> The body's life proceeds not, lacking work.
> There is a task of holiness to do,
> Unlike world-binding toil, which bindeth not
> the faithful soul; . . .

Continuing the pursuit of the sun's phases, we come now to Aquarius. This sign reflects the stage of life that is attained when once we are established firmly in our life's work. It may have been that the career (the word means, literally, 'a swift course'), swept aside opportunities to develop the more personal, creative talents and hobbies that may have been apparent in youth. Now, perhaps better placed to indulge individual interests, the mature adult can find a renewal of spirit in recreation (re-creation). At the same time, as befits one who has reached a point where much experience of life has been acquired and absorbed, there comes an inner urge to convey a little of that understanding to others.

There is nothing obscure in this concept; senior staff of hospitals give lectures to juniors, experienced members of commerce and industry instruct trainees, and parents impart hard-won wisdom of life to their offspring. (The latter, of course, in their vigorous, self-seeking, Leonian phase — the Zodiacal opposition — may be disinclined to listen!) The intimate and personal fires of Leo now find expression through the Aquarian Water Carrier, disseminator of knowledge.

Finally, the sun moves into Pisces, and the cycle is almost complete. Dissemination now gives way to diffusion of life principles, and personality becomes redolent with the collective memories of the past, yet is instinctively aware of the metamorphosis that is to come, and the new life-force that will again spring up as the cycle re-commences. Because of their intuitivity, Pisceans do not always take easily to the process of learning hard facts. They feel they just 'know'. The arduous task of having to think and reason things out, and deal with the practicalities of life, is something better suited to their opposite number, Virgo. As always, the struggle for polarization and balance continues.

The Zodiac, you will have realized, is rather like a mirror reflecting the whole of human experience. In it can be discerned the creation of the universe, the evolution of life, and civilization; man, from his primitive, elemental beginnings to the present, and beyond! In this brief interpretation of the Zodiac I have tried to present to you a distillation of the intricate whole, rather than the usual disjointed account of each sign. The complexities of the relationships between each sign, degree area, and degree, without introducing the additional complication of planetary interpretations, is quite staggering, but always fascinating and challenging to the intellect. Readers who are interested in astrological symbolism, and who would like to know a little more about it, might like to explore further with the aid of a textbook. A reliable, widely acclaimed introductory work is Jeff Mayo's *Teach Yourself Astrology*.

6. THE LIFE PHASES

One of the most widely used aids to forecasting in astrology is the 'One Degree Measure'. This is based upon the 'day for a year' principle, referred to previously. The concept is quite straightforward. In its annual cycle, the sun moves approximately one degree per day. This is an astronomical fact which was adapted by astrologers, long ago, in their observations of the apparent cosmic influence upon human affairs. By converting the sun's movement from one degree per day to one degree per annum, it was found that there was, in fact, a curious correlation of these broader sweeps of time with life trends.

The technique has been utilized from antiquity and is surprisingly effective in the 'progression' of the individual birth-chart.

Just to set the background to the Life Phases, I will explain briefly their derivation. At your time of birth the sun occupied a particular degree of the ecliptical circle, within the sign area which you will probably know by name, as your 'Sun-sign.' Each sign equals thirty degrees, so that if, for example, you were born at the very beginning of Taurus, on the 20th April, it is going to take, by One Degree Measure, approximately thirty years to traverse this sign before entering Gemini. When this change-over occurs a subtle alteration of expression becomes apparent. Here, for instance, the individual gradually takes on some of the mercurial qualities of the Geminian temperament, as an overlay to the basically deliberate Taurean type of expression.

In practice, not only the sun is observed in this way, but all the other bodies, too. The Moon, moving much quicker, passes through all the signs in approximately twenty-eight years, and subsequent variations of mood and response can also be perceived.

Clearly, a thirty-year solar period is rather too long for practical reference or interest, but within each sign further divisions, known as decanates, have been observed. These cover an area of ten degrees each, and impart their own particular modification to the overall qualities of the signs. Thus, each of the Life Phases represents a decade.

In describing the symbolism of the Zodiac to you, I have endeavoured to illustrate in a simple way how each sector relates to every other, not only as a sequence of development, one phase following another, but in their interrelationship as polar-opposites, as well as in their geometric, angular, and numeric structures — as seen in the cross (4), and the triangle (3). All, of course, are contained within this wonderful, vibrant, cosmic circle.

This marvellously integrated structure, a mandala of the soul, is, it should always be remembered, the conscious projection of mankind's unconscious and part-conscious experience of life upon the firmament; man ever reaches upward to discover himself in the Cosmos. With this, perhaps rather grandiose conception in mind, you will appreciate that any attempt at generalized interpretation is sadly inadequate. All that one can try to do is to convey a few of its implications in a way that, hopefully, has some relevance to the human condition. Fundamentally, we all respond to environmental conditions in much the same way, no matter what our colour, country, or creed. Thus, there is a common factor in the heart of humanity, and it lies in our basic feelings and responses. We behave the way we do because of the way we are, and will tend to respond to circumstances in a particular manner.

The Life Phases, therefore, refer to types of *probable* response in given periods. When I first investigated the sub-divisions of the signs I found that, in a curious way, they each contained an inner quality or tonal value — for want of a better description — that was extraordinarily similar to the four 'function types' of Jungian psychology. These functions are: thinking, feeling, sensation and intuition, and it is generally found that we each operate through our most dominant function, and that its opposite is usually the most troublesome, and therefore most likely to be projected on to other people. For instance, thinking types are prone to mistrust their feelings, sensation (i.e. sensible) types tend to be very wary about intuitivity, and vice versa. It is interesting to observe that Jung depicted these four qualities in the form of a cross, like this:

```
                    THINKING
                       |
   SENSATION ———————————+——————————— INTUITION
                       |
                    FEELING
```

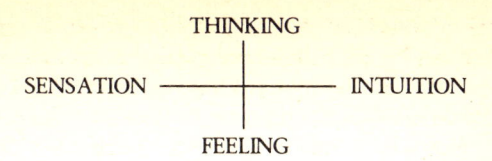

It is possible to go some way towards correlating these recognized psychological classifications with the signs, but the dynamics of the Zodiacal circle, like human behaviour, is far too complex to categorize in such a simplistic way. Even Jung was at pains to make clear that his four categories should not be considered as rigid divisions, but rather as a broad aid to the classification of behaviour patterns.

The essence of these functions is present, however, throughout the ecliptical circle, permeating, as it were, the twelve sign divisions, and modifying their expression accordingly. For example, to classify someone by their generally known Sun-sign characteristics only observes part of the sign picture. It would be correct to describe a 'Sun Geminian' as being either of a thinking, feeling, or intuitive disposition, depending upon which part of the month they were born in. Popular astrology only takes into account the general view that Geminians have active minds, like talking, communicating, thinking, and so on. Of necessity, these are limited views that do not do justice to this or any other sign interpretation. Needless to say, in the analysis of individual birth-charts the Sun's position is only one factor among a score of others, each of which has to be assessed and compared with every other.

Because, it seemed to me, that the observation of these functions adds a greater dimension to the overall picture than can be obtained from an interpretation of the general sign tendencies only, I devised a series of 'code words' to augment each phase description. These words are in italics, so it is easy enough to find their meanings in the Word Code Reference List. Under the four main function headings you will see various sub-headings. This is because it is virtually impossible to classify everything in black and white, and even four shades of grey are somewhat limited. Therefore, I have tried to account for some of the subtler combinations that present themselves (astrologically) as ecliptical polarizations, and which lend themselves to interpretation in accordance with known psychological tendencies.

For example, it is possible to see the astrological correlates to 'sex-drive', in the Zodiacal wheel, and yet this does not always externalize in the expected way. An individual, who, for whatever reason, is unable to satisfy this basic urge, may well direct this dynamic force into other areas of expression. The highest forms of spiritual and artistic aspiration, or the dedicated striving of the ambitious can all be external manifestations of the same basic yearning. Therefore, 'libido' is a more suitable word, especially when employed to convey the idea of a basic, physical-emotional energy, equating with a life-force, rather than Freud's limited view of it being only sexual energy.

Or again, thinking is a function that derives from ego-awareness and conscious effort. Simply responding to fleeting ideas and images that enter the mind is not thinking, but an automatic response to physical sensations or intuitive promptings from the collective unconscious.

Let us now see how the Life Phases work in practice. Ilie Nastase, Rumanian tennis champion, well known for his temperamental outbursts, though actually a rather shy man, was born on the 19th July. The sun was then in the 25th degree of Cancer, and you can find that his birth-date falls in the 20th Life Phase. Here, the code word 'susceptive' at once tells us that within the body of emotional response (Cancer), there lies a quality that can be classed under the thinking function, though extended through the imaginative faculty.

Turning to the Birth Date List we find that his 1st Phase change occurs at his 4th year of life. Each phase is of a ten-year duration, and so we can say that from approximately age 5 to 14, Ilie became fired with the urge to shine or succeed. We do know that he achieved much success remarkably early, and was already winning tournaments by the age of twelve. This confirms, very clearly, the 'Me first!' quality that colours this period, and its 'self-determining' motivation.

By the age of fifteen the 22nd Phase became operative, and now we can see a period in which, with growing confidence, Ilie is able to enjoy to the full what he is doing, and can therefore extend himself in his chosen profession. This is just the time of life when hope for the future prevails, and the idealism of youth buoys up the spirit.

The next change occurs at age twenty-five. This brings Ilie to the 23rd Phase, and now something more is required from life, no doubt, as we can see that while the boost of energy which is inherent in this period could be a useful reinforcement to his athletic capabilities, it is also likely that an 'active' questing or restless seeking arises, but for what? The fact that 'active' comes into the category of Feelings gives us the clue, and so it is no surprise to learn that at the age of twenty-six he married a young lady of a more reserved and quieter temperament than himself. Thus, it could be reasoned, he satisfied the need, of this phase, to experience a greater sense of concentration and restraint.

'Pop' idol Elvis Presley was born on the 8th January, which places his birth-date right at the beginning, in the 1st Phase, though by age four the change to the 2nd Phase takes place — as indicated by the Birth Date List. This tells us several things. The initial impress is one of some ambition, underlined by 'heightened feelings'. Referring to the Word Code List we find that 'libido' is involved here. Therefore, a deep urge, which in someone else could be expressed in some other manner, is, as it were, constrained, eventually to be re-directed.

Then, while Presley was still in his early years, the 2nd Phase takes over, further stimulating the urge to achieve through ambitious application, though this is now coloured by an expectancy. We know that he became interested in music at an early age, and learnt the guitar by the age of ten. During his teens, with the 3rd Phase covering the 14th to 23rd year of his life, aspiration becomes strengthened by a self-willed tendency, and so it was that Elvis started performing at the age of 19 years, and achieved considerable success by the age of 21 years.

During the decade of the 4th Phase (age 24 to 33 years), he was obviously riding the crest of his success, the 'mental alertness' and independent expression attendant to this period, with its quick, restless, yet sociable response, no doubt bringing out that jerky, quick-fire style that he made his own. Towards the end of this period, aged thirty-two years, he married, though this was not to last, and eventually ended in divorce. Perhaps it was that by this time the urgency or the 'libido' was less acutely felt, and an age had been reached when the natural instinct was to establish a more permanent union and way of life. Yet this is not really a phase that easily supports a pattern of unaltering stability, and it is as if Elvis had anticipated the phase to come, in which we see that 'feeling values' enter the scene.

This 5th Phase proved to be his last, for he died tragically young, at the age of forty-two years. As can be observed, although it tends to bring an emphasis to the feeling nature, it is not the easiest phase so far as emotional involvements are concerned, and with his manner of life, with all its tension and stresses, it would be reasonable to suppose that trying to recapture all the verve and sparkle of his earlier performances was too physically demanding.

I feel sure that with the foregoing explanation and examples, you will have a fairly clear idea how to proceed. To make things as simple as possible I have summarized the directions for using the Life Phases at the end of this section.

However, there are two points that need to be understood. Firstly, with regard to the ages indicated for the change-overs, these should be considered as close approximates. For the majority of readers they should prove relevant because I have based them upon the highest frequency of dates coinciding with the sun's transit from one sign to the next. The sun's movement varies very slightly, so that in some years the date of change differs. As many of you will know from reading your horoscopes in the magazines, some variation of sign is apparent for those who happen to have been born around the 21st of a month. This cannot be avoided because of the necessarily generalized approach. In individually calculated birth-charts, the sun's actual degree and minute of arc position is established from reference to the place and moment of birth.

Secondly, although I am sure it will be obvious to you, the Life Phases have been interpreted in such a way as to convey an impression of the type of responses likely to develop, but they must be viewed in relationship to the original birth pattern, and indeed, in the light of what you know of yourself, and your own particular life-style. Naturally, if you happened to have been born in the same period as Elvis Presley, this doesn't mean that you are going to be a pop singer, although you may well perceive some of the same kind of tendencies, i.e. personality traits, in your own character.

No birth dates have been given for the example personalities in the Phase List because it is human nature to identify with particular individuals, and the only reason for including them is to assist in presenting as wide a picture as possible of the various facets of human behaviour that may be apparent in any given period, either as inborn traits of the birth phase, or as trends or tendencies modifying the original potential.

Directions

1. Look for your birth-date in the Birth Date Table. Note the Phase Number at the top of the column. This corresponds with your Sun-sign sector, and you may already be familiar with some of its characteristics.

2. Note the approximate year of change, given in the left-hand column.
3. Remember that, apart from the initial Phase, unless your birth-date happened to coincide with the beginning of a Phase (when it too will be equivalent to a ten-year period), each Phase equals a decade of life, symbolically.
4. Note the words in italics and refer to the Word Code Reference List for additional interpretations of Phase qualities.
5. If, when following the sequence of Phases, you come to the end of the list, just carry on at the 1st Phase.

USING THE BIRTH DATE TABLE

1. Find your birth date.
2. Note the Phase number at the top of the column.
3. Observe the direction of the arrow.
4. Note the number of years to the Phase change in the left-hand column.
5. Each Phase thereafter represents ten years of life.

Explanation. Because the sun hardly ever returns to exactly the same degree position on the same day each year, there is a variation of approximately 3 degrees to be allowed for. Assuming that the majority of readers will not have an astronomical ephemeris, I had to devise a simple means to find the approximate position of the sun, and to allow for the variation. The birth date figures refer to the highest percentage, and therefore the majority of readers should find little or no adjustment necessary. The arrows indicate the direction of adjustment, usually by one day (year), though it is worth allowing for a second year's adjustment. The three longer arrows indicate where it may be necessary to adjust by two or perhaps three days.

Example. Age thirty-five years, and born on the 25th January. Birth is therefore in 3rd Phase (and should therefore read something like your Sun-sign interpretation), and the change to 4th Phase will be by age six years. The arrow indicates that it may be necessary to adjust down, i.e. to a changeover at five years of age. The remaining thirty years, to arrive at the current age, equals three Phases. Therefore, the change to Phase 7 is about due, or alternatively, in about one year's time.

Example. Age forty-two years, and born on 30th May. The arrow tells us that it may be necessary to adjust back by up to three years.

USING THE BIRTH DATE TABLE

BIRTH DATE TABLE

PHASE		1	2	3	4	4	5	6	7	8	9	10	10	11	12	13
		Jan							Mar							
YEARS	10	1	11 ↑	21 ↓	31 ↓	Feb	10 ↓	20	↓ 1	↓ 11	↓ 21	↓ 31	Apr	10	20	30 ↑
TO	9	2	12	22		1	11	21	2	12	22		1	11	21	
CHANGE	8	3	13	23		2 ↓	12	22	3	13	23		2	12	22	
	7	4	14	24		3	13	23	4	14	24		3	13	23	
	6	5	15	25		4	14	24	5	15	25		4	14	24	
	5	6	16	26		5	15	25	6	16	26		5	15	25	
	4	7	17	27		6	16	26	7	17	27		6	16	26	
	3	8	18	28		7	17	27	8	18	28		7	17	27	
	2	9	19	29		8	18	28	9	19	29		8	18	28	
	1	10	20	30		9	19	29 ↓	10	20	30		9	19	29	

PHASE		13	14	15	16	16	17	18	18	19	20	21	21	22	23	24
		May				June										
	10		10 ↑	20 ↑	30 ↑	1	↓ 11	21		3	↓ 13	↓ 23 ↑		3	↓ 13	↑ 23 ↑
	9	1 ↑	11	21	31	2	12	22		4	14	24		4	14	24
	8	2	12	22		3	13	23		5	15	25		5	15	25
	7	3	13	23		4	14	24		6	16	26		6	16	26
	6	4	14	24		5	15	25		7	17	27		7	17	27
	5	5	15	25		6	16	26		8	18	28		8	18	28
	4	6	16	26		7	17	27		9	19	29		9	19	29
	3	7	17	27		8	18	28	July	10	20	30	Aug	10	20	30
	2	8	18	28		9	19	29	1	↓ 11	21	31	1 ↓	11	21	31
	1	9	19 ↑	29		10	20	30	2	12	22		2	12	22	

PHASE		24	25	26	27	27	28	29	30	30	31	32	33	33	34	35	36
	10		3	↓ 13	↑ 23 ↑		4	↓ 14	↓ 24 ↓		3	↓ 13	↓ 23 ↓		3	↓ 13	↓ 23↓
	9		4	14	24		5	15	25		4	14	24		4	14	24
	8		5	15	25		6	16	26		5	15	25		5	15	25
	7		6	16	26		7	17	27		6	16	26		6	16	26
	6		7	17	27		8	18	28		7	17	27		7	17	27
	5		8	18	28		9	19	29		8	18	28		8	18	28
	4		9	19	29	Oct	10	20	30		9	19	29		9	19	29
	3	Sept	10	20	30	1	11	21	31	Nov	10	20	30	Dec	10	20	30
	2	1	11	21		2	12	22		1	11	21		1	11	21	31
	1	2	12	22		3	13	23		2	12	22		2 ↓	12	22	

Therefore, check Phase 16 and see if it accords with what you know of your own birth-sign tendencies. If not, try Phase 15. If this happens to fit, then it can be assumed that the change-over could have been between 1 and 3 years. Forty years of life accounts for four Phases. Assuming some doubt, this brings us to either the end of the 19th Phase, or just into the 20th. It is easy enough to check the interpretations of both.

As you can see, the procedure for our little experiment is very easy, and I trust it will prove interesting for you. As can be appreciated, it would be virtually impossible to tabulate the sun's daily position for, say, the past sixty years or so, and I had, therefore, to devise a system of reference, simple and easy to use. It provides an approximate indication of the likely change-over period, and allows for adjustment, either way, to account for the variability of the Sun's motion.

LIFE PHASES

1. There is an element of reserve, control, or responsibility about the qualities of this phase, albeit, with a sense of underlying drive that arises from *heightened feelings* coupled to self-determination. To some extent, and in some individuals, the affectional nature may be temporarily suppressed in order to pursue a particular ambition — the head ruling the heart. Elvis Presley, for example, achieved success at 21 years, though he did not marry until 32 years of age. Richard Nixon, one-time President of the United States, and also born in this period, exemplifies, perhaps, the ambition that is inherent in the underlying motivations of this phase. Both men provide examples of the struggle to achieve a balance between personal aspirations and relationships, whether personal or public.

2. There would seem to be a conscious need for application or concentration of mind, probably upon work and responsibilities, in order to achieve greater security. As progress is made through this phase it is possible for a sense of hopefulness to become more apparent. Overall, there is a greater likelihood of applying the self to the daily tasks or career with an *expectant attitude* for most of this phase. Thus, there can be a mixture of aspiration and inspiration to tune into. A time, perhaps, for careful thought for today, and visions of greater promise for tomorrow. In this context it is also possible to see the interplay between material and spiritual values. This is quite well illustrated in the life of A. P. Sinnet, who was a newspaper editor and Vice-President of the Theosophical Society.

3. For those who have been progressing with hope and aspiration, this phase may well see an increase of drive and desire to achieve some sort of recognition. However, the underlying motivation is likely to be of *a self-willed* nature, and this could produce a general restlessness. This, in turn, could lead to an exacerbation of stresses

in relationships, should any be present already, below the surface. H. M. Stanley, of "Dr Livingstone, I presume?" fame, was a journalist and explorer, occupations that kept him moving around the world for most of his very active life. The up-surge of a self-willed type of behaviour is probably most noticeable in the first year or so of this phase.

4. For those born in or who are moving through this phase, the tendency will be to become more *mentally alert*, and therefore it should be possible to perceive more rapidly, and consequently be better able to see opportunities that may be presented. Clearly, for anyone who may be carrying over the self-will of the previous period, this additional stimulus of mind is likely to provide a further spur to lively endeavour. Freddie Truman, famous Yorkshire cricketer, characterizes the independent personality who is also sociable and humorous. This, to some extent, conveys the general nature of this phase. Ronald Reagan, President of the United States, and one-time movie star, who has the same birth date (6th February), also exemplifies very well the social and humanitarian principles that are inherent in the qualities of this phase.

5. From the mental alertness of the previous phase there is now a shift of emphasis towards the emotional level. Therefore, *feeling values* may tend to colour the outlook rather more, with a consequent increase of response to stimuli. Some inclination to want to avoid what might be felt as the too restrictive influence of others may also be apparent. For some, born during this phase, self-will in love or a desire for independence could be evident. For others, able to accept the responsibilities and emotional involvement of relationships, a more restrained attitude will be apparent.

The life of King Farouk, born at the beginning of this phase, became that of a dissolute, while Sir Francis Galton, born towards the end of the phase, was a scientist, famous for instigating the use of finger-printing in crime detection. The sense of social awareness, apparent in the previous two phases, is carried over to some extent, but here we can see how the same type of underlying features can be so differently expressed. In the first, as self-gratification, and in the second, as a dedication of self to society. The third to sixth years of this phase may see some increase of responsiveness and activity.

6. In comparison to the previous phases, this period in a life could be marked by a heightening of sensitivity. The individual becomes rather more receptive to external influences. Those who happen to

be born during this part of the year may well evince a *susceptive* quality; their thinking is either greatly enhanced by an increased imaginative capacity, or they are liable to take a too diffuse view of life. The great novelist and poet, Victor Hugo, is a fine example of the imaginative and intuitive intellect that is embodied in the qualities of this period, as too is George Harrison, musician and song-writer, and one-time member of the 'Beatles'. Around the fourth year of this phase there may be a likelihood, for some individuals, to become rather more introspective or hypersensitive to conditions. Obviously, much will depend upon the age that this period is entered at, and the prevailing circumstances.

7. The sensitivity of the previous phase now takes on a more *responsive* quality, marking a time, perhaps, in which the tendency is a little more emotional than intellectual. It could be as though this is a time in which there is a growing need to crystallize what has previously only been anticipated through feelings or thoughts. Hence, both the affectional or artistic urges could be viewed against more material values. For example, marriage might appear to offer the required security, for some, or relationships generally take on increased significance. This is illustrated quite well in the life of Jean Harlow, Hollywood star of the thirties, who ran away from home and was married by the age of sixteen. Or in Michelangelo, whose whole life was devoted to bringing actuality to the outpourings of his artistic soul, and practicality to his architectural creations.

8. On moving into this phase an *intensification* of the underlying drives and emotional urges becomes likely. It is quite possible for the individual to become (or be) indefatigable in the attainment of his or her objectives. There is, perhaps, less caution than in the previous phase, with more likelihood of impatience and overstrain. For those born in this period it could be as though their aspirations reach to the heights. Liza Minnelli typifies the artistic passion and drive of this phase, while Albert Einstein's passion for science carried him to universal acclaim. (Students of astrology will be interested to learn that the mid-point derived from the third decanate of Pisces, and its polar opposite, produces: "A good mathematician" according to R. Ebertin, in *The Combination of Stellar Influences.* The method for extracting mid-points from decanates is outlined in my book *Stress and the Sun Signs*).

9. Entry into this phase can be associated with a marked stepping

up of energy. The individual becomes *active* and enterprising in the pursuit of success, or in achieving satisfying relationships. During the course of this decade, however, should the demands made upon others be too great, a certain amount of unrest could develop, especially so if the individual also becomes disputive. Over-assertiveness and hyper-activity could peak around the middle (fifth year) of this decade. The famous escapologist, Harry Houdini, exemplifies the enterprising and physically active person who can be associated with the period.

10. The energy of the previous phase now begins to take on a more *self-determining* quality, in which there can be a marked desire to assert in order to acquire recognition. Self-determination, here, is also bound up with either the artistic or affectional drives, so that some *intensification* of feeling, especially if involved in these areas, is also very likely. The personal attraction that can be expressed by those born during this period is well illustrated by Mary Pickford, an early star of the silver screen. Doris Day, popular singing star of the sixties, is another example of successful self-determining allied to charm, and she also shares the difficulties that strong individualism can bring into relationships, for both women married three times. Around the fifth year of this phase there may be a tendency to over-do or over-react, and therefore the encouragement of patience and tact would seem to be prudent.

11. Here, in this decade, it becomes possible to perceive a lively frankness of approach, and a refreshingly broad view of life that can be both constructive and humorous at the same time. Although this is probably most applicable to those born in this period, much of the motivation that can be derived from the phase arises out of the *idealistic* qualities that should be apparent. The self-assertiveness of the previous two phases can now be better directed into a wider sense of vision, as required, for instance, by any aspiring leader of others. Sir Charles Chaplin, who will forever be affectionately remembered as 'Charlie Chaplin', exemplifies the vigour, the directness, and the breadth of vision that is encompassed within this period.

12. The underlying colouring to this phase can be seen as *heightened feelings*, and some alteration to the general expression, in comparison with the previous phase, with its outgoing vigour, may become apparent. Here, there is more containment, with the feelings strong, deep and enduring. For those entering this period it

should gradually become apparent that there is now an overlay, as it were, of greater patience and persistence, augmenting, perhaps, the energetic pursuit of interests and objectives.

The quality of endurance that is imparted in this time may be observed in the dedication to office of Queen Elizabeth II, or in the complete professionalism of an outstanding musician like Yehudi Menhuin, world-famous violinist. Barbara Streisand, also born in this period, provides another example of the artistic soul who can become completely involved with the challenges of vocation.

13. Deliberation and intuition go hand in hand, and the feeling nature becomes enhanced by imaginative stirrings. Individuals born in this period may tend to rely upon their dreams and aspirations as an incentive to achieving their goals. Here, very often, the physical attributes of the athletic type combine with the imaginative powers of the poet or actor. Rudolph Valentino and Tyrone Power, both extremely popular movie idols in their particular eras, had a curiously similar type of physical attraction. This is probably not surprising, since they were born within a day of each other. For those who enter upon this period, the quality most likely to be imparted by it is one of an inspiratory nature, the mind possibly becoming more open to suggestion, and *expectant* in outlook.

14. The emphasis here is possibly upon material security, though modified by a feeling (for example, affectional), or artistic quality that seeks for physical satisfaction, either by way of creature comforts, or through the rigorous control or direction of the senses. We might say that those who are born into this sector of the ecliptic, have a great capacity to feel and to be aware. Two outstanding personalities who convey some idea of these features very well are British ballerina, Margot Fonteyn, a superb artiste, and no stranger to rigorous self-discipline, and Liberace, American pianist and highly successful entertainer, who clearly has combined the capacity for hard work with an artistic flair. It could be reasoned that the aspiration of the previous phase now has a chance of materialization in *sensible* endeavour.

15. This is a phase of greater movement and possible change. A need is felt, maybe, for altering and innovating, for seeking fresh interests to stimulate the questing mind and satisfy the curiosity. Those who happen to be born during this period may well wish to gain, and to demonstrate their intellectual skills, for they are

usually *mentally alert* and communicative people. Bob Dylan, American folk singer and song-writer, illustrates the versatility of this type, as too does the famous English actor, Sir Laurence Olivier. In their own ways they both evince a mastery of language, and the ability to communicate thoughts and feelings. For those entering this phase from the previous ones of a somewhat steadier tempo, it could be that there is now more mental restlessness, perhaps a little disturbing for those who had taken an unchanging, stable life-style for granted. It may be of help to consider that the key to this phase is adaptability.

16. Those born during this period are usually eager, alert, and ever seeking for acceptance. Although mentally very active, *feeling values* may now tend to dominate, with a resultant inclination to experience mood swings, for example, from elation to depression. There may also be a certain degree of self-consciousness inherent in the tendencies of this period. Judy Garland and Marilyn Monroe, both born in this time, and both so evidently eager, yet so vulnerable to the attitudes of others, show extremely well this sensitive balance between the bright intellect and the responsive feeling nature. Those moving into this phase may find that the confident spontaneity of the previous period now takes on a more introspective note, and greater consideration has to be given, perhaps, to relationships.

17. Alertness is now increased, perhaps to the point when, as it were, the mind drives the body, ever observant, and ever ready to react. There may be a great need for individual self-expression, and again, all the various modes of communication are likely to be called into operation. Famous film star Errol Flynn, whose somewhat erratic and colourful life demonstrates the restless striving for new, stimulating interests, illustrates clearly the *self-determining* type of motivation encapsulated within this phase. Likewise, Enoch Powell, British politician and brilliant intellect, again shows, by his chequered career, this restless seeking for mental stimuli and individuality of expression, so beloved by natives of this period. We might say that this phase is impregnated with an electric energy that either sparks the individual into new activities and endeavours, or else leads to a period of increased tension — depending, of course, on the challenges that life happens to be presenting at the time.

18. The sun moving into this phase of its symbolic cycle brings

about a swing, away from mental activity and towards emotional response. There is less of the self-independent seeking, and more of a conscientious caring type of feeling, the individual being highly *responsive* to the needs of others, and instinctively, if not consciously aware of the struggle between the outer world and the inner life.

Helen Keller, that most courageous American woman, who gave most of her life to the welfare of the handicapped, herself having overcome the staggering obstacles of blindness and deafness, is an exemplar of one who evidently must have lived through her inner life, yet was acutely aware of the needs of others. Or, there is another example of the same sort of tendency, yet expressed in quite a different type of personality. Barbara Cartland, romantic novelist, prides herself that she knows what the public likes, and, indeed, what is good for them! She is also a vigorous advocate of 'health foods'. Those who are moving into this phase may discern a greater sensitivity to the environment, and may tend to seek for greater security, love and comfort.

19. This phase may see an *intensification* of feelings, with the increased possibility of emotional restlessness. The strength of feeling can become a motivation to achieve, and very often those who are born during this time have a desire to feel causative in some way or other. Edward Heath, former British Prime Minister, rose from modest beginnings. He is an accomplished musician and successful yachtsman, though he remains unmarried. It could be reasoned that his 'libido' has found resolution in his public service and recreational activities. George Borrow, born in Norfolk, England, author and famous for his travels, took the deepest interest in the people of other countries, and the way they lived. He was also renowned for his great energy.

20. The emotional, feeling-tone still persists, now raised, however, and extended by the powers of imagination and intuition. People born during this phase can have a great deal of sympathy, being highly receptive to the feelings of others. This *susceptive* tendency may make for a vulnerability of feelings, leading to a desire, perhaps, to withdraw at times, into the imagination. A. J. Cronin, an author whose first profession was that of a hospital doctor, became famous for his classic novel *The Citadel,* which vividly expresses his own deep feelings and compassion for suffering society. Ilie Nastase, whose life trends we have already looked at, is clearly hyper-sensitive to the atmosphere of the tennis

court. Here we have an example of two apparently different types of personality; one an academic, and the other a sportsman. Yet both harbour the same acute sensitivity and receptiveness to external influences. We could reason, then, that the colouring of this phase is one of much intuitive understanding, and with a potential for compassion.

21. A reversal of attitude may take place upon entry into this phase. This doesn't mean that the "leopard will change his spots," but that some modification of outlook is possible. If, before, the approach to life was of a sympathetic nature, with thought for others, the present overlay may now prompt a more self-centring type of response. A *self-determining* urge could begin to develop. The epitome of the self-made man was probably Henry Ford, and, at a less constructive level, we have a good example — almost a caricature figure — of the over-inflated ego in the form of the strutting little Italian dictator, Benito Mussolini.

Needless to say, this does not mean to imply that everyone, either born during this time, or moving through it in the course of their lives, is going to experience ego-inflation. It is simply that it is a probable tendency which, if recognized, should be allowed for. As one leaves the imaginative aspirations of the last phase, it could be that this stage provides greater opportunity for a clarification of personal objectives, perhaps imparting more confidence. For those born in this period it could be that self-expression is of paramount importance.

22. This phase should extend the vision and the imagination. It is a time for confident, broad-scale planning, and involvement in social activities. Popularity, where sought after, becomes possible. People born during this phase often exhibit a marked *idealistic* quality which may seek to find expression in the arts. For example, outstanding poets like Rupert Brooke and Lord Alfred Tennyson, Poet Laureate. We find, too, highly competent actors like Dustin Hoffman, several times nominated for Oscar awards. Enjoyment and gaiety are also hall-marks of this phase.

23. Confidence and a sense of fun persists, with still a need for self-expression, but an initiating quality creeps into the picture, so that natives of this phase often manifest a great deal of energy, physically and mentally. Yet there is now rather more reserve or concentration of purpose than in the previous phase, with perhaps a touch of seriousness to the general demeanour. We might say that in this period there is an inclination to become *active,* probably in

an instinctive desire to gain a greater sense of security.

Exemplars of these tendencies are Princess Anne, and novelist Sir Walter Scott. In the former it is not difficult to see, from television reports and interviews, that there is much courage and conviction, and a purposefulness that is softened by a lively sense of humour, revealed, on occasion, by the well-known whimsical smile. Scott was a writer of extraordinary industriousness, the more so when spurred by the need to pay off huge debts.

24. Confidence in creativity and self-expression now give way to a reticence and practical disposition. The search for security is increased, and pursued in sensible, efficient ways, though with due regard for harmonious co-operation with others. Patience in mastering specialized skills or techniques, a quiet humour, and an *expectant* attitude are some of the qualities of this period. Film actor Sean Connery, best known for his James Bond role, was born in this period, as too was novelist John Buchan, famous for his *Thirty-nine Steps,* though he was also a brilliant scholar and notable statesman.

25. A little more serious than the last phase, with an even greater capacity for industry and thoroughness. It is probably conscientiousness that shapes the pattern here, so therefore there may be rather more inclination to worry over matters of detail. More consideration may be given to such interests as work, diet or health. For those born during this period there could be some underlying struggle when it comes to achieving satisfactory relationships. Examples can be found in the late Peter Sellers, and in Queen Elizabeth the First. The former's comedy antics masked a deeply serious nature. He was very prone to anxiety, and was unable to achieve a lasting relationship. The latter, of course, was known as 'The Virgin Queen'. It could be said that this phase should, or could be seen as one of *sensible* endeavour.

26. Commonsense now becomes allied to *heightened feelings,* and it is the emotional, inner urges that may threaten the practical intentions. If this proves to be so, we might see, for example, a striving to achieve balance between practical or ethical considerations and, say, the affectional nature. Hence, some difficulty in relationships would be a likely manifestation during this phase, but should by no means be considered as inevitable.

We find, in Greta Garbo a film star reputed to have said "I want to be alone!" — someone who gave up the struggle to relate to society, perhaps because of the sense of overpowering inner feelings which could have caused anxiety. Or, there is Sophia Loren, also born in this phase, whose diligence and hard work won her success as a film actress. She is also known for her marriage to Carlo Ponti, a man many years her senior, but to whom she has clung with great determination. Here, it could be reasoned that the inner motivating force of feelings has externalized as enduring affection.

27. With the entry into this phase we may see a swing towards increased social involvement. The company of others becomes more significant and meaningful, and greater co-operation is sought after. Those who happen to have been born in this time often express friendliness and affability. Typifying this quality is ex-President of the United States, Jimmy Carter. Because *feeling values* now enter the picture it is likely that, although adaptable and obliging in many respects, some struggle concerning the affectional nature may be apparent, as in some vacillation of feelings concerning close associations, personal or general. In the main, however, greater sociability would seem to be an appropriate consideration as a likely tendency or trend during this decade.

28. In this phase, sociability becomes injected with a *self-willed* colouring, so that although much friendliness is apparent, there is now a greater tendency to go one's own way, or in having a desire to be different. We might say that those who were born during this period are sociable yet independent, having a touch of self-esteem. They are, perhaps, a little reformistic, too. In British Prime Minister, Margaret Thatcher, we have a clear example of such characteristics, while in John Lennon, one-time member of the 'Beatles', independence-seeking and self-will manifested in his somewhat rebellious views, and unique artistic talent.

29. Social co-operation is the key-note and, for example, those who happen to have been born in the previous phase, may now have to come to terms with the necessity for adaptation and reasonable compromise, essential for all social growth and involvement. Those born during this period have a natural understanding of this requirement, and usually evince pleasant, friendly behaviour, with intuitive understanding of other people. They are imaginative and *mentally alert*. Cliff Richard, very popular singer for many years, whose natural friendliness has endeared him to audiences the world over, evinces this quality of lively understanding and awareness. There is sometimes a deep felt idealism about romantic interests.

Another man to provide an example of someone who was well liked, and who was a great diplomat with deep understanding of humanity, was Dwight Eisenhower, President of the United States, and Supreme Commander of the Allied Expeditionary Force during the Second World War.

30. A tenacious striving to attain selected goals could be the type of trend associated with this phase. It is a decade of *intensification* of underlying urges, and natives of this period usually seek for deep, emotional fulfilment, albeit with a sense of maintaining control. Arch-manipulator of the deeper emotions was Joseph Goebbels, Nazi Minister of Propaganda. At the end of the Second World War, when, no doubt, he felt that both he and his country had lost effective control, he took the extraordinary step of killing his family, and then committing suicide. At the other end of the scale, though still harbouring powerful undercurrents of emotion, we find Dame Sybil Thorndike, great English actress. She could express intense feeling in her performances, was a stickler for discipline in her work, and preserved an air of dignity and reserve throughout her life.

31. Perception in depth is the colouring to this phase, for now the intensity of feelings, which tend sometimes to centre the attention upon the self, gives way to a sensitivity that imparts an intuitive understanding. Natives of this period are often imaginative and *susceptive* to the feelings of others. There can be a distinct sensitivity to emotional stimuli, as evinced by the life of Edward VII born near the end of this phase. Alternatively, we can observe, in the life of scientist Marie Curie, pioneer in the field of X-rays, that there is a quality of an investigatory nature; a curiosity, or interested probing and searching into unknown realms.

32. Vigorous and ambitious striving is possible in this phase, which has about it a hint of ruthlessness, especially when an individual is set upon achieving a particular objective. *Responsive* to challenges, individuals born in this period can demonstrate a marked audaciousness, yet they are instinctively aware of the need for direction and control. This interesting combination of purposefulness and caution is well illustrated by the life of Billie Jean King, American tennis champion, reputed to be intuitive and highly emotional, but who, nevertheless, has so clearly driven herself to success by dint of self-discipline and unflagging ambition. Likewise, famous German Commander of the last war, Rommel, showed

immense skill and dedication throughout his brilliant military career.

33. The last three phases have about them a quality of introspection, and therefore individuals who have been moving through them for up to thirty years or more, may find that entry into this phase brings a certain amount of unrest to the feelings, in one way or another, for now the tone is one of outgoing expansiveness, with a generosity of attitude. Far-reaching plans, imagination, and an *idealistic* approach to life are some of the characteristics to be found in those born in this period. The tonal quality of this phase is therefore one in which there is a desire to extend the mental horizons. Mark Twain, for instance, had the spirit of wanderlust from an early age, besides being a prolific writer. Sir Winston Churchill's breadth of vision, mastery of language, and high idealism, carried Britain to victory in the last war.

34. A marked vigour and mobility often relates to those born in this period, along with a display of enthusiasm in whatever they do. The principle of *active* participation which is inherent to this phase, may, though probably more apparent in those born during this period rather than those who are moving through it, tend to be an instinctive counter measure to cover feelings of insecurity or inadequacy.

Walt Disney's abundant 'animation' was poured into his cartoon characters, and one wonders if Mickey Mouse, with his lively appeal and cheekiness, alternating with an endearing hesitancy and shyness, was a projection of Disney's own personality traits. Certainly, he was a perfectionist, and overconscientiousness can sometimes be a compensatory action for anxiety about one's capabilities. Frank Sinatra, highly successful as a singer, has not had the smoothest of passages in his relationships (see *Word Code Reference List* for expansion on 'active'), either personal or professional. Thus, the general trend within this decade would appear to be one of restless endeavour, with a certain amount of competitiveness.

35. Restless enthusiasm now takes on greater purposefulness as a more *self-determining* quality establishes itself. Nevertheless, there is kindness and good-heartedness to be found in those born at this time of year. Such features may be readily observed in the personality of Eamon Andrews, British television personality, best known for his programme *This Is Your Life*. Similar tendencies can

also be discerned in the life-style and manner of Noël Coward, famous for his acting, plays, and musicals. Truly a man of the theatre, his talents were extraordinarily wide, and there is no doubt that he was large-hearted and generous to his friends. This is a decade, perhaps, in which to grow mentally and spiritually, and to seek new opportunities.

36. Enthusiastic purposefulness now gives way to dour industriousness. Those that enter this phase may find it necessary to adjust their tempo of life to one that is a little more serious or restrained than hitherto. Those who were born in this period of the year are usually of a *sensible* nature, capable of much hard work and application to their responsibilities. There is a tendency to concentrate thoughts to the extent of becoming rather one-sided. However, there is a marked sense of reserve or diplomacy here, and not a little humour below the surface, if sometimes a mite caustic. American President Woodrow Wilson, and British Prime Minister W. Gladstone, were born within a day of each other (not in the same year, of course), and both were clever mimics! They were also both remarkable for their diligence and oratory.

N.B. If your birth-date places you near the end of this List, just carry on at the 1st Phase.

If any noticeable 'effect' is apparent, it will usually occur in the first year or so of a transition from one phase to the next. Changes which prove to be most noticeable and maybe a little more troublesome to adjust to than others, occur when the transition is between two signs of widely divergent characteristics. For example, from Sagittarius (Phases 33, 34, 35) with all its broad idealism and expansive outlook, to Capricorn (Phases 36, 1, 2) with its sense of constraint and serious application.

After a year or two into a new phase, it is as if the individual begins to 'tune-in' to the tendencies of that phase, and life feels more settled again. Where there is an obviously easy and natural transition from one phase to the next, and if the phases happen to coincide well with the actual age and development of the individual, evolvement of personality, leading to fulfilment — in so far as any one can achieve this in a lifetime — should be a reasonably smooth process. However, it is wrong to be too complacent; those who achieve most in life are often the ones who experience the greatest challenges.

If you find that your Life Phases appear to be relevant to your own broad experience of the past, there is an obvious advantage in being able to consider your current Phase, and the one to come. With this additional insight into the sort of trend or background colouring to your responses, you will be in a better position (a) to utilize underlying motivations that may not have been discerned previously, and (b) accept and work with, rather than fight against, the perhaps uncomfortable feelings of new Phase tendencies.

WORD CODE REFERENCE LIST

1. THINKING FUNCTION

INTELLECTUAL MODE

Mentally alert. There is usually a clear emphasis upon mental activity. The underlying motivation is, therefore, the desire to communicate, exchange ideas, and to gain co-operation. Hence, a useful period for developing intellectual interests, conducting business arrangements, social and group involvements.

Idealistic. Intellect now becomes stirred and extended, and has about it a rather more diverse and restive quality, as though reaching out in an endeavour to find opportunities for greater understanding through a more active, personal exchange with others. Thus, qualities such as large-scale planning, generosity, frankness in the manner of speech, and a confident, more optimistic outlook on life, are able to find expression in this decade. Underlying motives probably arise from a desire to understand, and to be understood, or in finding ways to command or capture the acceptance of others.

IMAGINATIVE MODE

Expectant. Here, thinking relates more to the senses, resulting in a springboard effect, so that aspirations are stimulated by the need to find answers to problems, in the hope of achieving greater physical ease or security. Therefore, this should be a decade in which the mind, perhaps spurred by practical necessities of life, extends to encompass wider concepts than hitherto. That is to say, the broad concepts of idealism which instigates the planning process, have now to become visualized as more clearly defined thoughts and images in the mind's eye. Thus, with clearer ideas crystallizing into actuality, the coming ten years could see a gradual improvement in the mode of earning, work operation, or productivity. Hence, the tendency to proceed with practicality and expectancy.

Susceptive. Here, mind is related to the emotional responses, and whereas, previously, the inclination was to derive hope from practical or material concepts, there is now a tendency to become over-imaginative, if anything, and inspiration may be sought for within the dream-world of fantasy and imagination. This then, may be a decade when it becomes necessary to keep a firm grasp on all main objectives, in order to lessen the likelihood of uncertainty and indecision.

2. FEELING FUNCTION

PHYSICAL — EMOTIONAL MODE

Feeling values. Clearly, the implication here is fulfilment of the sexual urge, though the emphasis is upon harmonious co-operation, friendliness, love, adaptability, and so on. In the wider context, there is a sense of friendly associations, the enjoyment of popularity, greater social involvement. Therefore, it could be supposed, for example, that the next ten years are conducive to the forming of close liaisons, love affairs, marriage.

Active. Still has a sexual connotation, but now with more restless activity, and some degree of assertiveness, perhaps, in the pursuit of physical satisfaction. More heat and passion is implied here. Motivation probably arises from the instinctive feeling that the right sort of activity will result, hopefully, in the desired outcome. In general, this decade could be said to be one in which there is greater emphasis upon energy expenditure. A good period for the sportsman, or the athletic lover!

LIBIDO. EMOTIONAL — PHYSICAL MODE

Heightened feelings. Sex-drive now becomes a more deeply felt thing, sensual, and perhaps bordering on the obsessive, in some cases. Co-operation is sought for, in order to obtain complete fulfilment, emotional or material. This powerful inner-force, comprising emotional strength and physical energy, most readily finds an outlet through sexual feelings. Though, since it relates to a deeply contained drive, aligned with the senses, it may well surface in the form of over-riding ambition; a need to master the environment in some way. Hence, this could be a useful decade for greater achievement in the career, and for consolidating one's position.

LIBIDO. EMOTIONAL MODE

Intensification. This implies a particular concentration of the emotional force, or libido. It relates, here, almost entirely to the emotional side of personality, and may take on any form of outer expression, and not necessarily that of a sexual nature. Because the strongest and most intense urges arise from the deepest recesses of the psyche, externalization directs the attention to areas of interest that have an element of profundity about them. These can range from the occult or hidden, to the aesthetic and erotic, from the highest spiritual aspirations, to the fathomless depths of the human soul. Naturally, the full potential of the libido, as indicated in this context, will be most marked in the behavioural tendencies of those born during the Phases and periods containing the word 'intensification'. For those moving into this ten-year period, it is possible that an increase of tenacity and striving for particular objectives will become apparent. We might say, too, that there could be an intensified pursuit of emotional and physical fulfilment.

3. SENSATION FUNCTION

Responsive. This word is intended to suggest what appears to be — astrologically, at least — an interesting blend of sensibility and emotional response. The type of personality category it most closely resembles is Jung's 'sensation type', but with a touch of the feeling type, too. Hence, there is a need for security and comfort, and a degree of responsiveness that brings out a sense of responsibility in those who care for others. Because of this apparent alignment of feelings or responses to the senses, it could be reasoned that this decade sees a potential for care-taking, conscientiousness, and striving, though with some susceptibility, perhaps, to swings of mood, or anxiety.

Sensible. Just as 'responsive' leads to responsibility, so does 'sensible' imply sensibility, a product, for the most part, of the sensation function. Sensation brings about a conscious awareness of one's self and one's environment. ''The sensation type remains with things'' observes Jung, ''He remains in a given reality.'' Such types have an abhorrence of the irrational, and view themselves as being rational, practical creatures. They, are, however, just as vulnerable to their senses as thinkers are to thoughts, or feelers to their feelings. In this decade, therefore, with a growing emphasis upon physical sensations, it may be that material values, and bodily functions, i.e. health matters, come to the fore. The motivation is probably one of taking a 'sensible' attitude about life and work; maybe wanting to achieve more tangible results from industrious effort.

4. INTUITION FUNCTION

Self-determining. Persons who act intuitively have insight and immediate apprehension of any given situation. Not for them the well-defined boundaries, beloved of the sensation type. There must be freedom to move and react. There must be opportunity to rely upon their own initiative, and scope for purposeful action. This, then, is a decade for enthusiastic endeavour and bold undertakings. Time now to shrug off introspection and uncertainty.

Self-willed. Rapid reaction to environmental stimuli is usually present in good measure. There is often a lightning-like perception bordering on the inspirational. A progressive mentality and originality are usually evident, though with all this restlessness of mind, and the continual seeking for fresh interests, there may be a danger of scattering the energies. In this decade, probably, there is an impatient seeking for acceptance as an individual, and a desire for greater authority or significance.

Whether or not you can accept the precepts of astrology, I trust you have enjoyed this light introduction into a profound subject, and that you may have been intrigued by our little experiment in time. Hopefully, you will have been encouraged to read further.

Astrology, although founded upon the most deep-searching and philosophical concepts that mankind is capable of, is not a religion. However, anyone who studies the subject, even for a short while, cannot fail to have his or her understanding of the inner world of the psyche raised and expanded considerably. Astrology is an extension of awareness at the mundane level, assisting externalization of the contents of the unconscious, personal and collective, by helping to clarify the archetypal images and symbols.

The symbolism of the Zodiacal Circle may be considered as a living, vibrant thing. It encompasses patterns of becoming which form in the passage of time, to become inscribed upon the unconscious of humanity by the ever-spiralling Cosmos.

May I leave you with this thought:

> Trust the PAST to the mercy of God,
> The PRESENT to His Love,
> The FUTURE to His Providence.

Anon.

BIBLIOGRAPHY

Arnold, Sir Edwin, *The Bhagavad-Gita*, Routledge & Kegan Paul Ltd., 1961.
Anderson, M., *The Secret Power of Numbers*, The Aquarian Press, 1972.
Bono, Edward de, *Lateral Thinking*, Penguin Books/Ward Lock, 1970.
Dunne, J. W., *An Experiment with Time*, Faber & Faber Ltd., reprinted 1953.
Ebertin, R., *The Combination of Stellar Influences*, Ebertin-Verlag, 1960.
——, *Transits*, Ebertin-Verlag, 1971.
Forman, J., *The Mask of Time*, Macdonald & Jane's, 1978.
Franz, M-L von, *Number and Time*, Rider & Co., 1974.
Harrison, M. J., *Fowler's Compendium of Nativities*, L. N. Fowler & Co. Ltd., 1980.
Hone, M., *The Modern Textbook of Astrology*, L. N. Fowler & Co. Ltd., 1964.
Iverson, J., *More Lives Than One*, Souvenir Press Ltd., 1976.
Jung, C. G. *Analytical Psychology*, Routledge & Kegan Paul Ltd., 1968.
——, *Modern Man In Search of a Soul*, Routledge & Kegan Paul Ltd., reprinted 1981.
——, *The Undiscovered Self*, Routledge & Kegan Paul Ltd., 1979.
——, *Synchronicity*, Routledge & Kegan Paul Ltd., reprinted 1977.
Jung, E., and Franz, M-L von, *The Grail Legend*, Hodder & Stoughton, 1960.
Mayo, J., *Teach Yourself Astrology*, The English Universities Press Ltd., new edition 1980.
——, *The Planets and Human Behaviour*, L. N. Fowler & Co. Ltd., 1972.

Needham, J., *Science and Civilization in China*, Vol. 3, Cambridge University Press, 1959.
Rudhyar, D., *An Astrological Mandala*, Vintage Books, 1974.
——, *Astrology and the Modern Psyche*, CRCS Publications, 1976.
Sewell, R. J., *Stress and the Sun Signs*, The Aquarian Press, 1981.
Whitrow, G. J., *The Natural Philosophy of Time*, Thomas Nelson and Sons Ltd., 1961.

INDEX

active, 81, 85, 89
An Experiment With Time, 7, 8, 15
Analytical Psychology, 25, 29
Anderson, Mary, 20
'Angels of Mons', 56
Aquarius, 58, 62
   Age of, 28, 54, 55
Aquinas, St Thomas, 29
Aries, 52, 57, 58, 59
Augustine, St, 28, 29

Bhagavad Gita, 62
Bible, The, 28
biorhythms, 18
Bloxham Tapes, 15
Bridey Murphy, 15

Cancer, 58, 59, 68
Capricorn, 45, 58, 61, 62, 86
Castle Acre, 14
'change of life', 51
Christ, 28, 61
Christianity, 20, 30, 54
Christmas, 61
Collected Works, (Jung), 42
Combination of Stellar Influences, The, 76
computers, 53-4
Correlation, 41
cosmobiology, 22
cosmogram, 22, 39
counselling, 34

de Bono, Dr Edward, 19
De Civitate Dei, 28, 29
decanates, 66
divining
   boards, 37
   rod, 24
DNA molecule, 24
dowsing, 25
dreams, 15, 16, 21, 30, 40
drugs, 17
duality, 20-1
Dunne, J. W., 7, 8, 15, 18, 19

Ebertin, Reinhold, 22, 49, 76
Einstein, Albert, 11, 19, 76
expectant, 74, 78, 82, 88
extra-sensory perception (ESP), 18, 24, 33
Eysenck, Prof. H., 41

Falkland Islands, 49
fate, 8
'Father Time', 44-5
feeling
   function, 89
   values, 75, 79, 83, 89
Fleiss, Dr Wilhelm, 18
Forman, Joan, 13, 14
fortune-teller, 23, 30
future, 19, 23-6, 92

Gauquelin, M., 41
Gemini, 52, 58, 59
'Great Cycle', 50
'Grim Reaper', 45

heavenly bodies, 28, 29, 42
heightened feelings, 74, 77, 82, 89
hexagrams, 23, 24
Hone, Margaret, 52
Horary astrology, 51-2
'House' divisions, 53
'Human Condition', 56
hypnosis, 15, 17

I Ching, 23, 38, 43, 51, 52
idealistic, 77, 81, 85, 88
Industrial Revolution, 55
intensification, 76, 77, 80, 84, 90
intuition function, 91
Iverson, Jeffrey, 15

Jackson, Glenda, 48
Jeans, Sir James, 31
Jones, Marc Edmund, 52
Jung, Carl, 20, 21, 24, 25, 29, 31, 32, 36, 67
Jupiter, 28

Law of Relativity, 19

Leibniz, G. W., 11
Leo, 58, 59
libido, 68
Libra, 57, 58, 59

Man and His Symbols, 40
mandala, 66
Mars, 28, 40, 50
Mask of Time, The, 13
Mayo, Jeff, 41, 46, 49, 64
Mayo School of Astrology, 34
memory, 17
mentally alert, 75, 79, 83, 88
Mercury, 28
Middle Ages, 47, 51
Modern Man in Search of a Soul, 29, 60
Modern Textbook of Astrology, The, 52
Moon, 18, 21, 28, 40, 43, 50, 65
'morphic resonance', 31, 32, 42

Nastase, Ilie, 68
New Scientist, 31
Newton, Isaac, 11
Nixon, Richard, 74
numerology, 20

'out-of-the-body experiences', 32, 33
Oxford, 30

past, 13-17, 19, 92
Phenomena, 27
Physics & Philosophy, 31
Pisces, 28, 58, 63, 76
   Age of, 28, 54
Planets and Human Behaviour, The, 46
present, 17, 19, 92
Presley, Elvis, 69, 74
'progressions', 42, 49, 50
psychology, 34, 48

recession, 61
reincarnation, 15
religion, 33
responsive, 76, 80, 84, 90
Rhine, Dr Joseph, 18, 19, 31
Rudhyar, Dane, 52
runes, 43
Russell, Bertrand, 11, 17

'Sabian Symbols', 52
Sagittarius, 58, 61, 86
Saturn, 28, 44, 45, 46, 48, 49, 50
Science and Civilization in China, 37

Scorpio, 58, 60
Second World War, 25
'Secondary Directions', 48
Secret Power of Numbers, The, 20
self-determining, 77, 79, 81, 85, 91
self-realization, 35, 62
self-willed, 74, 83, 91
sensation function, 90
sensible, 78, 82, 86, 91
'Serial Time', 19
Sheldrake, Rupert, 31
Sinnet, A. P., 74
sleep, 17
Solarscope, 53
Stress and the Sun Signs, 7, 9, 40, 52, 76
Summa Contra Gentiles, 29
Sun, 18, 21, 28, 43, 49
sundials, 37, 38
susceptive, 76, 80, 84, 89
swastika, 38
Swoboda, Dr Hermann, 18
symbolism, 22, 25, 28, 43, 48-9, 55, 62, 63, 66
symbols, 20, 45, 56
   status, 57
'synchronicity', 31

Tao, 38
Tarot cards, 23, 24, 43, 51
Taurus, 52, 58, 59, 60, 61
Teach Yourself Astrology, 49, 64
Teltscher, Alfred, 18
Thatcher, Margaret, 49
thinking function, 88
'time slip', 13, 14, 15, 30
Transits, 49
'transits', 42, 49, 50

'UFO', 56
Undiscovered Self, The, 25, 36
Uranus, 51

Venus, 28, 40, 48, 50
Virgo, 28, 58, 60, 61
von Franz, Marie-Louise, 19, 20, 21, 24

'Wise Old Man', 46
Woodruff, Maurice, 44
'work ethic', 61

Yang, 37
Yin, 37